To ARVID VATLE

a fellow pilgrim
in the search for the Truth

I gladly acknowledge my debt to the
Rev. Canon Horace Dammers, architect
of the 'Common Discipline' of Coventry
Cathedral, and to Mrs. P. H. Holmes
for her help in preparing the manuscript.

H.C.N.W.

Contents

Contents

1

Perspectives of a Changing World

A DUTCH AUGUSTINIAN, Father Adolfs, in his book *The Grave of God* has coined the word 'rapidation' to define the characteristic of the age. It is a good analogy. History is seen to flow like a great river, carrying the commerce and communication of human society, providing the means for cleansing and refreshing humanity as it flows uninterruptedly on its historic course.

From time to time the river changes its level of flow, and flows in confusion and at greater speed down the rapids from one level to another. Its course is broken by jagged rocks, whirlpools and much froth.

The period of history in which we are living is very accurately analogous to the tumbling rapids of the river. It is important to get a perspective of history, to see the present in relation to the past, and to set a course for the future. Undoubtedly there have been periods of history when change was evolutionary, steady and predictable. Many may resent the passing of that calmer life. Many may try to hold fast to it and avoid the rapidation of change. The present tension between the conservative and the progressive, the traditionalist and the radical is the tension between two different perspectives of history. This is true of political attitudes, whether in Britain or Czechoslovakia; but it is no less true of attitudes towards change in the life of the Christian Church. This book is a plea for greater tolerance of the experimental, for greater understanding of the radical. Leadership of Church at every level, when the river of history flowed smoothly, required qualities of a particular kind. Those qualities are not adequate to steer the craft down the dangerous rapids of change.

The man or the group in society which can hold its canoe on course down the rapids will be the man or group in society which will emerge to provide leadership and elicit loyalty when the river again flows on a smooth, strong course. Such a man or group must keep its nerve, avoid being drawn into the whirlpools of confusion, dashed against the rocks of despair or blinded by the froth of much superficiality.

It is helpful to apply this analogy in as much detail as possible to the life of the Church as we experience it, whether at the national, local or personal level. There is a grave danger in the Church as a whole, and among Christian individuals within it, of our losing our nerve, of our being confused as to our course, and of our being suffocated in much superficiality. There is a general sense of despair abroad. We speak of the collapse of civilisation. We fear the collapse of the basis of religious belief, and nod sagely, when we hear our times described as 'post-Christian'. We sense impending doom, and fear lest we are being led to the edge of revolution and anarchy.

These are essentially the rocks and whirlpools of the rapids of history at any time of change. It is pre-eminently the responsibility of leadership in State, in Church and in every sphere of education, to distinguish the true from the false, the real from the superficial, and to develop a perspective of history which gives hope and not despair.

It is tempting to labour the obvious implication of the futility of trying to avoid going down the rapids, and to stand poised on the brink of the tumbling waters pretending that the river is still flowing smoothly, in spite of all the evidence to the contrary.

It is not necessary to castigate the Church alone for such obscurantist conservatism. The Church is often accused of being medieval by politicians and educators who would do well to look to the medievalism of their own systems before they accuse the Church of refusing to change itself.

The fact is, of course, that the whole of society tends, in its panic at the suddenness of change during a period of rapidation, to resist change by every means. Whether in the faith and order of the Christian Church, or in our ponderous parliamentary system, or in the plumbing system of our homes, we find it easier to discover reasons for not changing anything than we find to discover the wisdom and courage to come to terms with change.

Later it will be necessary to consider the scientific and technological character of the 'rapids' of change, and to consider the widening gulf between technocrats and people.

Rapidation, therefore, is the first feature of the

perspectives of our changing world which we must note.

The second is the perfectly evident one that we are living in a period of greater change than the world has ever known in a comparable period. Before this observation is written off as too obvious a piece of current jargon to need repeating, it is worth analysing some of the specific changes which have occurred. These changes have been in many instances the particular points of pressure upon *theory* – political, sociological and moral – with which the Christian must come to terms. Paloczi Horvath, in his book *The Facts Rebel,* rightly points out that in speed of communication and travel, in the penetration into the nature of matter, the nature of space, and the nature of man himself; in the conquest of diseases, in techniques of birth and death control – in all these and many more, the world has advanced further in the past 25 years than it has done in the previous 4000 years.

This aspect of the anatomy of change does not need labouring, but it requires noting at the beginning of this consideration, so as to understand the uniqueness of the period of change in which we are living, and the uniqueness of the tensions and pressures on established structures and theories. Failure to understand this uniqueness has led to almost suicidal despair, particularly among the older generation. A longer and more hopeful view of the historical context within which change is taking place depends upon an understanding of the quite unprecedented speed of change through which we are living.

Horvath further makes the point that because of the speed of change, theory — whether political, sociological, economic or religious — is under pressure from the facts. These facts include the over-population of the world, the great divide between the 'haves' and the 'have-nots', the confusion of the irrational and outdated international financial systems, the growing integration of national systems of industry and technology, unmatched by a growing integration of culture or education.

Theory is increasingly under pressure from the inexorable facts of this time of movement in human affairs. Theory is apparently less able to control the march of events. The rationalisation of the surrender of theory to the pressure of the facts leads to the current defence of 'pragmatism', 'consensus decision-making', 'keeping-the-options-open' in politics, and to 'situation ethics' among those who question the absolute validity of moral principles.

The same surrender of faith to events has evident dangers in the current fashion to seek God in the affairs of the secular world. Richard Jones's hymn *God of Concrete, God of Steel* does not err, as do many ballads and much theology, in omitting to place our concern for God in our contemporary world in the hands of the *God of history*. Too many of the modern definitions of God have nothing whatever to do with the God of Israel, though they may find some verification of Christian humanism in the relationships sought for in the name of Jesus Christ. It is right to try to understand the purpose of God in his ongoing creation, and to identify the compassion

5

of Christ with good works in our social life. It is right also to be aware of the danger of rationalising fashion and situations of change in terms which are vaguely theological. There are periods of history when it is more than usually necessary to be clear as to which is *vox dei* and which is *vox populi,* and this is one such period.

The surrender of theory to the pressure of the facts has created something of a crisis for democracy. We appear to be under two menacing pressures. The one is the pressure from above downwards, the pressure of dictatorship or of arrogant burcaucracy. The second is the pressure from below, the pressure of protest, revolution and anarchy. At the heart of the protest of the young generation is a valid cry for a preservation of what is honest and real, and a questioning of the arrogance of impersonality in the structures of government and administration which control us.

Between these two pressures is a dangerous vacuum. It is within this vacuum that there is germinated the crop of jargon which hides, beneath its monotous repetition, deep concern and frustration. 'Participation', 'dialogue', 'involvement', 'communication', are some of these. They are protest words out of the vacuum which define the characteristic of longing for honesty, for coherence, and above all for personal identity in an increasingly depersonalised society. It is out of the darkness of the vacuum that we must learn to understand the despair of our age.

For the third aspect of the anatomy of change

which specifically concerns the Christian it is helpful to use the analogy of the world of computers. To be efficient the programmer must programme the machine with certain basics and with certain variables. It is basic that one plus one will always equal two. I assume that the calculation of my bill for the supply of gas to my house will be accurate because it is based on that constant fact. The wages of the worker in the gas plant will change under pressure from other changing circumstances. Facts of this sort will be variable and, unless the Gas Board is to lose more money than usual, will be subject to constant scrutiny and result in regular reprogramming of the relevant computers.

The computer correlates the coefficients of both basics and variables that are fed into it, and produces a 'feed-back' which is the answer that is required of it in any specific inquiry. The efficient programmer will regularly examine the 'feed-back', and test its relevance to new conditions, social, economic, political, military, whatever the context of the computer operation may be. An adjustment is made if necessary, the computer reprogrammed, the 'feed-back' studied, related, and so on.

If an honest assessment is made of the part played by the Church in history, and especially in the development of European culture and social behaviour, it is valid to use this analogy, both to the credit and the discredit of the historic Church.

The Church has for centuries past, and eminently in the centuries following the Dark Ages, 'programmed' the secular world with principles, both

7

basic and variable. Principles of justice, mercy, compassion, the value of individual personality, principles of honour, courage and self-control are among the basics on which the Church's concern for human society has insisted. The humanist is less than honest in imagining that these virtues, which are basic to our civilisation, just happened on their own.

A study of societies which have attempted to dispense with a religious belief at the heart provides evidence in the face of which it is impossible honestly to assert that such moral virtues just happen on their own. It is fashionable to minimise the contribution of the Church to our historic civilisation in Europe. This can only be achieved by flying in the face of massive evidence to the contrary. Our educational system, our compassionate society, the care of the vagrant, the aged and the discharged prisoner, our systems of justice – all these derive from the care of Christian people.

Such a claim does not in any way minimise the horrors of the Inquisition, or the stupidity of the Church in Britain at the time of the Industrial Revolution or before and after the Reform Act of 1832. Nor does it underestimate the Church's guilt in failing to enter the social and industrial revolution taking place about us now, and so having less influence than otherwise she might have done in filling the vacuum of 'leaderlessness'.

But let the negative not obscure the positive. The Christian can take heart from the great achievements of the Church in Europe in providing leadership at times when political and social systems failed to do

8

so. The emergence of Christian leadership out of the decay of the Roman Empire, the great monastic movement which led Europe out of the barbarism of the Dark Ages, the great social and religious reformers of the fifteenth and sixteenth centuries, the Christian socialism of Wesley and his contemporaries, the rousing of the social conscience in the last century by the Salvation Army and great Christian socialists in the established Church — all these are glimpses of the ability of a Church, at a period of historic need, to provide leadership. It is not without significance that the communist histories find distinguished places in their record of social advance for Martin Luther and John Hus.

To return to the analogy under consideration. The Church has indeed 'programmed' the secular world. The process of studying the 'feed-back', relating it and reprogramming is essential to efficiency and accuracy. The man who defined the discipline of cybernetics, Norbert Wiener, insisted that cybernetics should provoke human beings to a greater understanding of 'human being' and not a lesser; to a greater understanding of that dimension which is peculiarly the character of being human, as opposed to being merely a mechanistic mass of actions and reactions, of reflexes and responses. He insisted further that unless the machine prompted man to a greater understanding of his own identity as a human being with powers of moral choice, then it was soberly predictable that within a generation, the machine would be cleverer than Man.

It is difficult to resist the view that, because of the

Church's failure to study the 'feed-back' from the secular world which historically it has programmed, and because, therefore, it has failed to 'reprogramme' the secular world as times have changed, the machine has 'become cleverer' than the programmer. The secular world has 'become cleverer' than the Church.

The Church finds it too easy to hold to past structures, too easy to define variables as basics, too difficult to distinguish the one from the other. In times of challenge and change, there are not lacking those who answer by reaffirming the old dogmas, reasserting the old structures, and resisting change by 'playing for time'. In the face of obvious needs to change or to redefine, theologically, liturgically and administratively, the impatient are expected to be comforted by the assurance that a 'Commission has been appointed', 'a Report is being studied', 'a Committee is about to be selected'. In the crisis of Christian education in the past 25 years, for example, it is alarming that no strategic aims have yet been declared to make certain that in the next generation there is a strong body of informed Christians to form the effective Church.

Recent declarations by Pope Paul under pressure of the need to change, make depressing reading at a time when there is everything to be gained by relating the 'feed-back' of questioning and doubt which come loudly and clearly from the secular world, to a re-examination of the truths which are at the heart of what we believe.

But let the Church take hope from the movements at its heart, in the cities, in work among the young generation, in some cathedrals and many parish Churches. Where honest attempts have been made to set free from the stalemate of tradition and barren dogmatism the study of what is true and relevant to the questions of our age, the response has been pentecostal in its power. The movement towards change is at the grass-roots level. It is nurtured by the needs of people where they are – in community life, in industrial structures, in schools, in the cultural changes taking place around us, and most of all in the pressing needs of individual people to resist being depersonalised by contemporary pressures. It is unfortunate that the leadership from above, both in the administrative structures of the Church and among those who govern the Church, tends to be cautious, mediocre and uninspired.

So much for the third characteristic of the perspective of the twentieth century within which a Christian must define his faith and brace his resolution: The Church is the 'programmer' of the secular 'computer' and must be ready to study the 'feed-back' in order to re-programme the computer for more relevant information and more efficient response.

A fourth aspect of the changing world is the obvious one of the population explosion and all the problems, tensions and fears which result from it.

It is, however, interesting to recall that in the mid-thirties a popular subject for debate in Britain was the adjustment of British society and economy to the forecast that, owing to the falling birth-rate, the population of Britain would be 15 million by the end

11

of the century. Now, owing to the increased post-war birth-rate and the falling death-rate, a population of 80 million by the end of the century is forecast.

While not denying the necessity to take precautions and to study the social problems of urban congestion, it is worthwhile to recall the fallibility of statistical forecasts. The danger is that highly imaginative forecasts of megalopolis and buildings a mile high could lead to panic legislation. We could very easily ignore the primary needs of persons, and legislate and plan for a massively impersonal society. No matter how complex or congested the cities of the future may be, the primary need will continue to be for simple human relationships providing personal security at the heart of the society.

While we are warned to anticipate a city stretching from Manchester to Marseilles, from Boston to Washington, and are told of vertical villages already on the drawing boards; and while we are being pressed by its very presence and inevitability to regard the motor car as our master, and ourselves as its slaves, it is easy to lose heart and to say that such a problem is too big for us. Human personality could very easily be regarded as a necessary casualty in our super-planned society of the future.

Who can say with confidence, however, what the effect of new drugs and fertilisers, and new contraceptive techniques will be? Who can venture to affirm that there are no unknown diseases lurking in the future move which our antibiotic-saturated bodies will be powerless to resist? Who is bold enough to chart a course of unimpeded population growth in the face of nuclear power, pollution of the air and sources of food on earth and in the sea, as more and more nuclear waste may well be deposited without adequate safeguards against its future effects?

History has a way of defeating human forecasts. Whether these forecasts are right or wrong, it will be well to get our priorities right, and to make it clear that whatever the structure of human society may be, what Christians are committed to safeguard is the supreme worth of human personality, and the value of every person in the eyes of God. From this basic principle, we are then committed to safeguard the basic principle of family life, which we believe to be the only true safeguard for the growth in love of human personality known to human society. The moment we forget this and allow ourselves to be hypnotised by spectres of impersonal monsters dreamed of by visionary town planners, we shall set our course towards the society envisaged in George Orwell's *1984* when the person counts for nothing and the impersonal power of monstrous bureaucracy counts for all. Many things at present lacking in our society will be added unto us if we 'seek first the Kingdom of God' in Christian family life in our homes.

There is an inbuilt urge towards identity in every person. There are those who argue that there is an inbuilt urge towards anonymity. This is not so. Whether in a kindergarten class, in an industrial organisation, in a Church congregation, in a city's population or anywhere else, there is an inbuilt longing in everyone to be identified as a person, to be

13

recognised for one's self.

This truth has become pressingly urgent at the level of racial identity. If we have an inadequate theology of the individual it is likely that we shall have an inadequate theology of racial identity. The uncertainty of policies in nations where black and white meet is heavily conditioned by the panic caused by fears for an overcrowded future, and by no means guided by a compassionate theology of concern for all as persons in the eyes of God.

Our modern cities dramatise another problem of the population explosion, namely the retreat into specialisation. No doubt this is symptomatic of the urge to find smaller, definable groups within which one can establish one's identity. There are dangers in this. The specialist tends to live in his own vertical 'tower of Babel' and to communicate vertically with other specialists in their tower, using jargon which is comprehensible only to themselves, and incomprehensible to other specialists doing precisely the same in their own 'towers of Babel'.

It is a common experience to find in our cities no effective communication between the town planner and the economist, between police and doctors, between engineers and educators, between politicians and priests. Equally in a university this is evidently so. The economist has no effective conversation with the moralist, the scientist with the historian, or the philosopher with the mathematician. Each tends to regard his own specialisation as containing the whole truth, and as capable of answering any question on any subject that may be addressed to it.

The Christian Church could make the same contribution to this situation of fragmentation as it has made in past periods of change. Society today has a great need for the touch 'that makes whole'. That touch is required of the Church. As in the centuries after the Dark Ages, the Church could rise to the need of the moment and provide centres for coherent communication. Such communication must be horizontal as well as vertical. The common ground between specialisations is an important area of necessary dialogue. At the centre of that common ground is a concern to rediscover the nature of man.

The fifth characteristic of twentieth-century change with which the Christian must come to terms is the so-called 'knowledge explosion'. There are more young people who are educated now than there have ever been at any one time in history. The standard of education is being raised each year, as qualifications earn a higher premium on the employment markets. Many are educated to a high standard of knowledge only to find that the world around them has few points of entry giving opportunities to apply their knowledge in a way which satisfies their hopes. Many others have abilities which cannot be accurately measured by a qualifying examination, and in consequence they are denied a higher education in which they can develop the special gifts which they have.

The result is the frustration which has become familiar in student and post-student behaviour. The restlessness will certainly increase as employment demands higher technical and scientific qualifications at the same time as mechanisation of skills, previously mastered by human hands and brains, constricts still further the opportunities for employment. This will create problems whose solution will require imagination and tenacity. The increase in hours of leisure could mean either an increase in the 'bingo' culture, or the creation of opportunities for a cultured life unrelated to the hours of necessary employment to earn a living. The Church has an opportunity to use its relationship with local communities in its parishes, and its much under-used 'plant' to provide significant leadership in the direction of leisure culture.

The knowledge explosion, however, demands clear response from Christian theology to the questions raised by the inquiring minds of the highly educated young generation. The theological debate which followed *Honest to God* has not abated. Study groups, youth conferences, house-parties, lectures and regular discussions are among the techniques for continuing the debate used by all progressive centres. These are a proper acknowledgement of the diminishing role of the pulpit in the teaching ministry of the Church.

The retreat of the Roman Catholic Church from exposure to the honest inquiry of the young generation into a reassertion of its traditional dogmas is one of the most disappointing reactions in contemporary Church history. If we have any confidence in the words of Jesus that he would 'send us the Holy Spirit who would guide us into all truth', we would do well to enter the great debate with faith and confidence. If God is truth, and truth is in God, as we believe, it is odd that we are afraid to expose our understanding of the truth to criticism and examination. It is our very confidence in the reality

16

of God who is the truth into which we may be led which should enable us to welcome a probing analysis of our theology, even to the extent of crossing the borderline of risk into areas of heresy, in order to verify our understanding of what we really believe.

Elsewhere in these pages will be a reference to the disastrous consequences of not accepting the challenge of the 'God is dead' philosophers of the period of the German *Aufklarung,* which finally discredited the traditional theology which took root in medieval times. The failure of the Church then, and since then, to encourage its people to understand the debate and to enter it, and not to insulate themselves against it, has again in our times created a situation in which the traditional Church has not been able to lift a finger to calm the sudden storm which greeted such books as *Honest to God.*

The exposure of religious philosphy to the need to be precise in playing its part in the contemporary intellectual debate, is compelling religion to be precise and thoroughly honest in the language it uses to communicate religious truths. To say that the concept of God is beyond human intellect and cannot be defined in intellectual terms is a perfectly defensible position that anyone can hold, but it prevents any sort of intellectual dialogue. We must be prepared, if we hold this view, for stalemate in the debate with those whose language is precise. Nor is the dilemma resolved if we try to force God into the intellectual, spatial forms familiar to scientific discussion, in which words have very precise meanings and evoke clear and recognised images.

17

BASICS AND VARIABLES

In order to establish the religious hypothesis in terms wider than spatial and physical, we must identify the area about which we are speaking.

2

Knowledge and Belief

THE pressure of this rapidly changing world upon religion has been great. The response of religion has been varied. While the frustration of patient efforts to unite the Christian Churches continues, there has emerged a greater coherence between all theistic religions. This is inevitable in view of the increasing polarisation of philosophies about the nature of the universe. The most important issue to be debated now is that which distinguishes from one another those who hold a mechanistic view of the universe, and those who hold the religious view of a second dimension — personal and spiritual — actively at work within the mechanistic framework.

If religion is to re-establish any sort of leadership of human destiny, it must establish this point with absolute clarity and confidence. To believe in the 'two-dimensionality' of the universe, in the sense used above, is basic to every theistic system of belief. Until that view of existence has been established, a theology of God will rest upon uncertain foundations.

It is at this level that the real religious debate is

being conducted. It is the basis of the ongoing
Marxist-Christian dialogue. It is at the heart of
the debate in the universities and schools. It is the
source of the questioning and the honest agnostic-
ism of a majority of intelligent men and women
who want a deeper foundation for the faith in a
God. They are searching for a clear definition of the
basic religious assumptions within which the
existence of God is a tenable hypothesis which can
be verified – or falsified – by their experience. No
unity among those who hold a religious view of
existence will be possible unless their unity on the
basic assumption of the 'two-dimensionality' of the
universe is clearly articulated. What will be accepted
as basic thereafter will vary according to national
characteristics, intellectual capacity and personal
temperament. But at this moment in history the
debate demands clarity about the basic truth that the
world is more than the sum of its physical parts, and
man more than a neuro-muscular system, that
reflected in his personality, in his moral sense, in his
consciousness of himself, in his awareness of life
pulsating in the universe around him, is an 'image' of
the universal Personal Presence whom we define as
God.

Then let the debate be more clearly understood as
it progresses through biblical study and history.
Conducted in harmony with all theistic religions, it
might lead to an appreciation of the extent to which
the influence of culture, history, tradition and
temperament have made the battlefields of religious
conflict in the past essentially battlefields of variables

and not of the basics they were held to be, for which millions have died in man's religious history.

The debate, however, is likely to be frustrating and fruitless unless we overcome first the difficulty of the same words creating different mental images in the minds of the debaters. It is necessary as well to identify clearly the area of experience which we claim to be beyond that which can be scientifically verified.

What, then, do words mean? What makes our mental images valid? How do we verify them as true? It is of fundamental importance to religious people that they are honest about this. Inescapably in our thinking aloud both in the pulpit, in our prayers and religious discussions, in our using words as instruments to express our fumbling faith, certain statements are made experimentally. In the absence of any other way of stating them, they become, for those who utter them and those who hear them, statements of dogmatic certainty. Other disciplines have their own jargon, but on the whole recognise their experimental and exploratory nature; and, on the whole, religion does not. Medical science has long since, for example, forsaken the dogmatism of the last century, in favour of open-ended progress through continual experiment. In contrast, experimental insights of liturgical worship in the sixteenth century are still the basic insights enshrined in the latest attempt at radical reform in the liturgy of the Church of England.

Let us now consider some examples of categories of words and phrases:

'The Sun is Shining.' This is, on a sunny day, a

statement of fact. Unless you want to indulge in philosophical games with words it is unrealistic to attempt to prove that this is not accurately true. How do I know? By experience. I can see it. I can feel it. I can see the results of it in other people and in nature. It would require more knowledge and more experience than I have yet encountered to disprove the fact that the 'sun is shining' is indisputably true.

'Napoleon lost the Battle of Waterloo.' I was not there. But it is possible by reading the accounts of those who were, by tracing the consequences of this event through subsequent history, by visiting the battlefield and finding relics, and by seeing artists' impressions of incidents in the battle - by all these it is possible to use history and its method to prove that this statement is true.

'I love my son.' This is something which is precious to me. It is something of which you may be able on the perimeter to see evidence, but it is something which is peculiarly mine. I alone can verify this. I alone can know whether this statement is an hypocrisy or not; and I am aware of it through processes in my own emotions and my own reflex actions when my son is with me. I alone know that this statement is true. There is a whole range of experiences which are of this sort which are precious to each one of us. We know whom we really love. We know whom we despise. We know whom we trust. We know whom we distrust. These are factual statements, but they are limited to our own experiences and are verifiable only by our consciences.

I can — and here I quote from Arnold Toynbee —

report what I find in myself and can compare my findings with my neighbours' reports of their findings about themselves. But if the reports disagree, the truth is not verifiable. A human being cannot enter into another human being's psyche to ascertain whether the other human being's report of what he has found there is correct in the opinion of an independent observer from outside. There is no way of ascertaining that one man's report about himself is correct and that another man's report about himself is erroneous.

This is even more relevant to the next statement: 'God is Love.' Now a person of unquestioning piety would undoubtedly say 'Yes I can verify this by all three tests that you have applied. By my experience of God's Love, by the historical evidence of God's Love, and personally by my own sense-reaction to this proposition.' But there are, equally, those who would find in both experience, history and their sensory response, evidence to confirm precisely the opposite view. Now I do not want to labour this. I think it is very clear from our own experience that 'God is Love' comes into conflict with those who deduce precisely the opposite from certain experiences — agonising personal experiences, cosmic experiences of great disaster, war and so on. And there are those who in their fumbling efforts to find the true meaning of prayer in time of great adversity will claim that their own experience denies this proposition. Now this requires careful examination as it is the basic of basics so far as religious affirmation is concerned.

Most of the confusion about religion is, I believe, due to our failure to identify the valid area of the physical and the valid area of the non-physical; the area within which experience and history and sensory reaction are valid arbiters of what is true and the area within which they are not. And most of the confusion is due to our obscuring rational thinking about spirituality by confusing our images and pressing too far the analogies that we use.

The human brain and the human neuro-muscular system is one of the living systems which are part of the natural law of control of the universe and of which we are a part. This system gathers experience and, through that experience, knowledge, on the basis of its own life-span of experience, and also on the basis of the accumulated experience of our predecessors in man's progress through life. Some of the safeguards of the ethical system in our society which, challenged though they may be from time to time, tend to reaffirm certain tested affirmations which become so basic in their validity for a healthy society that there are those who argue that their validity is absolute.

Now knowledge that we gain by experience is empirical knowledge. It increases with accumulated experience and is therefore relatively greater than it was 100 years ago or 1000 years ago. But it is not only relative in a chronological sense. *Knowledge is also relative to the dimensions of knowledgeability available at any one moment*. Now although that is a clumsy sentence it is essential to my argument. There is clearly a vast, conceivably limitless, area of knowledgeability at any one moment beyond our area of comprehension at that moment. This can be illustrated by the limited visual input of the retina of the eye and the further compression of what is received through the eye, depending on greater or lesser intelligence. It is still further compressed by the known fact that the average person only uses 5 per cent of the brain's capacity at any one time. The universe and the whole range of existence is therefore far greater than our sensory receptors can ever receive; and when they receive what they receive, it is only in a very minute and compressed form.

There are whole areas of understanding which man has quite inadequate perception to grasp – areas of whose existence we know only because of our perceptive experience of their results; life is one, love is another, suffering is another; so are courage, justice, truth. We can only perceive the perceptible action which results from the facts of their existence.

The brain computer consists of something like 10,000 million neurons. It is quite a lot. But even if we were to use all those neurons (and we do not, we use only 5 per cent of them) it is *the lot*. It is all we have. We have no more. It is the limit beyond which we have no capacity to go. The brain can only perceive up to the limit of its dimensions and not beyond it. Beyond it is an area of reality which we are not equipped fully to understand except through such evidence of its existence as is brought within the range of our normal systems of perception.

This violates a generally accepted – though entirely romantic — view of knowledge which assumes that the pursuit of knowledge has no limit and that ultimate reality can be comprehended by human knowledge. This is a purely romantic view and must be totally rejected by those who are looking for an honest definition of basics.

It is the way of the fundamentalist in his way, and the pietist in his way to try to compress religious truths into the same imagery and the same certainty as other forms of basic knowledge. It may well be that religious basics such as 'God is Love' and 'God has shewn mercy on me', are verifiable in terms of experience and history and sensory reaction. It is not, however, in this area that one must look for the validity of their truth, but in the area of BELIEF.

When I say 'I believe in God the Father Almighty', etc., I am not saying I know that there is a God, in the same way as I can say I know that the sun is shining today, because the basis of verifying one of those statements is quite different from the basis of verifying the other. Belief is placing one's faith in a system which experience teaches us has more answers to the questions that we address to it than any other system. The religious debate throughout history has been the testing of the system of belief called religion against other systems, political, philosophical and so on; and to religious people the religious system of belief still provides more answers to the questions addressed to it than any other system.

Does this, however, mean that the dogmatic utterances of the Creed represent a final statement of the elements of that system and that they are indisputably true now and for all time? Is truth static? Does it expand? Are there, in fact, certain basic principles which do not change?

Dr. McCulloch of the Massachusetts Institute of Technology sums up the human inquiry in this way. He says there are ultimately only two questions which must be asked. 'What is a number that a man might know it?' and 'What is a man that he might know a number?' He goes on to say the answer to the first of these. 'What is a number?' we know. And on this certain knowledge we have built our whole system of computing. But the answer to the second question, 'What is a man?' we do not know yet.

Now the basis of the sort of knowledge which is categorised as that which can be fed into a computer, which really embraces the knowledge verifiable by the first three tests that I have suggested — experience, history and sensory reaction — is the basic fact that one plus one equals two, and the whole computing system is simply a multiplicity of variations on this theme. Now in the second question 'What is man?' are there basics? Are we sufficiently certain that when the psychologist and the geneticist and all the others have analysed man they can dispose of man in the same basic terms as the cybernetician can dispose of the variations on the theme one plus one equals two? When he has finished, does this exhaust the question, 'What is man?' If so, it will be very difficult for religion to find any place for itself. But if not, as I believe without the slightest hesitation he will not, then how are we to approach knowledge in the area

27

which is beyond the capacity of the objective scientist to define?

Absolutism, in science, whether physical, chemical, mathematical or social science, is generally rejected today. But no less is it generally rejected in terms of religion. Honesty compels me to say I am only prepared to make statements in the belief that as far as I know up to this point those statements are probably true. I must subject them all the time to the probe of inquiry and honest doubt to make perfectly certain that those statements remain true in changing circumstances.

It is necessary to reflect for a moment on the place of doubt in the emergence of Christian belief, for no perspective of this world of change can ignore the widespread doubts which are probing the foundations of tradition, of culture, of religion, of civilisation itself.

The story of Tobias in the Apocrypha provides a delightful analogy of the companionship of belief and doubt. Young Tobias is summoned by his father to return to the homeland and to claim a family heritage. In the charming mythology of this old story, a companion (who happens to be an angel) is chosen to prepare with Tobias for the journey. One of the Bible's very beautiful verses marks the beginning of the journey: 'So Tobias set forth, accompanied by an angel and a dog'. And so it is with all honest people who journey purposefully through life. The angel drives us on to ideals and actions despite ourselves. The dog is ever present to test the angel within us, reminding us of the animal nature which is part of our human nature. The tension between these two is creative.

Another short contribution to this pen sketch of the creative role of doubt. A friend in Chicago established his sons in business. One developed a machine-tool business, within which he perfected an electric drill which made him a small fortune in a short time. He was, however, too content with his invention, and a rival studied his drill and found that he could improve it. This he did, and drove my friend's son out of business as far as that electric drill was concerned. My friend's comment on this was, 'Every belief must be accompanied by a doubt'.

Yet another feature of the place of doubt is suggested by the passage of Moses and the Israelites through the Red Sea during the Exodus. The Israelites had been in Egypt for 430 years – about the length of time that we stand from the Reformation. During that time they had become integrated into the social and economic life of Egypt in much the same way that Christian identity has become almost inextricably merged in the social and economic structure of our day. In the middle of the Red Sea, with the pursuing Egyptians pressing the Israelites to return, and the Israelites themselves nostalgic for the security of the 'devil they knew' in the past, as opposed to the 'devil they did not know' in the future, Moses himself appears to waver. 'Stand still,' he says, 'and see the salvation of our God.'

This is the all-too-common reaction to the moment of doubt, or the moment for decisive courage. The Church calls a Conference, appoints a Committee,

BASICS AND VARIABLES

issues a 'prepared statement' or awaits an impending
Report, which normally inhibits any action of any
sort whatever. So it is with parliamentary reaction to
times of change or challenge. How many Royal Com-
missions have been appointed in the last 25 years, the
result of which has simply been to 'shelve' action, and
to prevent any adventurous step forward? In the
Exodus analogy, God's voice thunders from heaven:
'Wherefore criest thou unto me? Speak unto the
children of Israel that they go forward.' This is a
significant moment in the passage of belief to greater
understanding of truth. It is required of us in
moments of doubt or challenge, or in moments in
history when we need to change direction, that we
sort out precisely what the relationship is between
our belief and social, political or theological fashion.
It is important that we are sure of the real roots of
our traditions, the *real* basics, and that we do not
confuse the variables of fashion with the basics of
established truth. In every period of change *vox
populi* tends to become *vox dei*, and never more
dangerously so than in these days of the worship of
the ideas enshrined in the much misused word
'democracy'.

The cybernetic distinction between basics and
variables adds another helpful analogy to this sketch
of the place of doubt in Christian belief. In science
we acknowledge that there are certain basics, like
gravity, thermodynamics, relativity, and many more.
Theoretically, these can be changed, and research is
constantly probing their truth. But many of these
concepts which are accepted as basics have stood the

test of all doubt and inquiry so far, and are still found to be able to provide confident answers to any questions addressed to them. So it is with the place of dogma in Christian belief. Theoretically they must be accepted as being capable of change. They are like signposts on the path up a mountain.

I well remember climbing a mountain to the north of Spitzbergen in 1938. As the mountain appeared not to have been climbed before, I had to find my own way up, which with the difficulties of summer ice and snow in Spitzbergen, and the crumbling rocks which are characteristic of the summer thaw, made progress slow and hazardous. After several attempts, I managed to find a safe way up. I collected a piece of driftwood from the shore, and hammered it in to indicate that this was the way up that mountain. A short time later I happened to be in that same bay and to my initial dismay found that my signpost had been moved to another place by some other climber. But I had to concede that his way up was a better way than mine.

So has the progress through the centuries up the mountain of Truth been marked; by concepts being proposed and tested by experience and philosophy and logic, to the point at which a concept could be accepted as a basic, and stand the test of any inquiries that may be brought to bear upon it. These concepts are among the basics enshrined in the creed, though there are many who would wish more probing to be directed towards the possible 'variability' of some of the credal statements which refer to the Church and the Ministry. None the less, provided the Church is

31

not afraid to be as honest in regard to its basics as is science in regard to such basics as gravity and thermodynamics, and is prepared to concede that theoretically they are subject to re-definition, then a great many more people would not cast away all belief for the sake of a small grain of doubt, as they are all too often compelled to do by the dogmatic arrogance which associates doubt with disbelief.

If the Christian is to maintain confidence in his belief in this age of questioning and doubt, then he must be encouraged to regard religion as a framework within which he believes he will find more answers to the questions that he addresses to it than any other framework. Religion will be for such an inquirer the framework within which he can enter into a living dialogue with the ultimate mysteries of existence and the nature of man.

Failure to accept doubt as a necessary stepping-stone to faith has led to the Church and large areas of our political and social systems 'digging themselves in', and building defences against progress and change. Failure to accept the creativeness of doubt has led to stagnation in our liturgy, in our theology and in the structure of the Church.

Our society is undoubtedly suffering both socially, politically, internationally, and theologically, because the basic ideas which are enshrined in some of the basic words that we use have been lost and diffused by the accumulation of variables which have been allowed to grow over the centuries. Basic concepts have been so obscured by variables that now they are wide enough to fit any rationalisation of any prejudice, any situation or any misunderstanding.

One has only to mention the word 'democracy', the basic idea of which is that the people should have a say in the guiding of their own destinies, for it to be clear that there is no word which is so capable of diametrically opposite meanings as this word is today, because it has been allowed to accommodate the pragmatic needs of any political situation to the point at which the word itself is prostituted.

'Freedom' is another such word. The original meaning of the word both in pre-Christian classical and religious writings and in the mind of Christ was 'freedom within discipline'. As my young son put it in reflecting on some disturbance in his classroom: 'You can only feel free if you can feel protected inside a wall of discipline.' And he did not realise that his mental image which was then confined to the classroom was one of the great cosmic truths.

'Peace' is another word; it can mean the absence of war, but the legitimate continuation of conflict without bombs. It can mean freedom to impose your own will upon somebody else. It can mean the conditions within which the stronger can flourish and the weaker can go to the wall. It can mean the very opposite of the great and glorious Hebrew concept of *Shalom* which meant the peace within which a man can commune with himself and with God.

I need waste no time on the prostitution of the word 'love'. The love of the television and film screen, or the love of the advertiser's imagery, is a different sort of concept from what we mean by the love of God. But at the heart of this we know that

33

love means a complete mutual self-surrender of persons to one another in love and trust. 'Truth' is a word which is capable of the same sort of distortion.

All this is obvious; but it is of cardinal importance in this age of the rediscovery of basic truth, that theology should expose itself to the same ruthless inquiry as to what is at the heart of its belief and what is variable around it. Consider the concept of the 'Resurrection'. The heart of the spiritual truth that life is total; that human life here on this limited spot called Earth is just a microcosm within the cosmic eternity called 'Eternal Life'; that there is no possible comprehension of life being limited in time and space; that human life, bearing within it the power of self-consciousness and therefore the highest form of conceivable life, cannot opt out of the continuity and eternity of life merely because we do not understand what happens beyond the grave.

But the accretions to this basic truth, which the resurrection of Jesus Christ (which we do not understand but which we accept intuitively and naturally as being true) in some way demonstrates, are all part of the urge to constrict this supernatural truth within the tests of natural verification (experience, history and sensory perception). So we tend to be forced to condition our acceptance of the truth of the resurrection by our acceptance of the detail of the tomb, the angels, the gardener, and, what is more devastating, the treatment by various artists, throughout the centuries, of this theme. None of these add anything to the intuitive acceptance that whatever happened, and however the people may have been led to

34

communicate what they experienced, the basic truth is that the whole Christian faith depended upon, and found its basis in, an apprehension of the fundamental truth that life is eternal and that the grave does not end it. One could – and should – apply this method of searching for the central heart of each part of our belief, and to every article of the Creed.

What, then, can be accepted as agreed 'basics' to serve as a hypothesis for proving the religious view of existence? At this stage it is sufficient that we are content with what is primary, indeed what the religious teacher has a right to claim to be basic assumptions.

First, that the universe is personal as well as mechanistic.

Second, that human perception is limited in proportion to the limitless scope of what exists in the infinity of space-time.

Third, that man is a fallible creature. The humanist view that believes in the fundamental goodness and limitless ability of human nature is romantic nonsense.

Fourth, that man left to himself tends to selfishness.

Fifth, that man has a 'conscience', in whatever form we may either explain it or try to explain it away. From within, man is conscious of an authority which defines certain moral imperatives in his behaviour.

If man is in any conceivable sense 'made in the image of God', then the first phase of the study of God is man. There are grounds for hope that much

35

study – scientific and sociological as well as theological – is finding common ground in a study of the
nature of man. In this study it would be surprising if
the 'basics' which emerged were not immediately
recognised as being essentially theological in their
implications Then the way would be clearer to
knowing what precisely we mean by 'God'.

3

Modern Alternatives
to Belief in God

WE BELIEVE that man can take some comfort from
the knowledge that centuries of attack against belief
in God, including assertions of the 'death' of God
(which go back nearly two centuries before the
present fashion to assert it,) and the widespread
disenchantment with, or passionate hostility to, the
institutional Church, even to referring to the Church
as the 'grave of God' – that all these put together
have not quenched man's hunger for the emotional
reassurance which an objectively centred religious
belief can give. For all our contemporary scepticism
and anarchy, Christianity has, as the twentieth
century draws to its close, no effective replacement
in western man's search for a religious synthesis of
his hopes and beliefs. Western man is still searching
for a religious faith. No honest philosophical,
psychological or socio-scientific studies can, with
intellectual integrity, ignore this fact of the human
condition.

This is, however, also to say that religion must be

purified of its accumulation of obscurantism, dishonesty and hypocrisy; that it must cast away much of its outworn cultic mythology; that it must identify the 'basics' of belief and be prepared to cast away many of the 'variables', many of which have been the cause of mighty battles in the past. Dr. Julian Huxley writes: 'Today we must melt down the gods, and refashion the material into new and effective organs of religion.' But Huxley's alternatives, 'free thought, free speech, freedom for physical and cultural pleasure, enjoyable friendships', usually found high among the values propounded by humanism, evade the question as to how those values can be pursued without the corruption which experience shows always accompanies the pursuit, and how they can be conducive to human well-being if they are not secured by a sense of the sacred. (see David Edwards, *Religion and Change,* S.C.M. Press)

This superficially attractive humanist philosophy begs too many of the questions posed by human experience to be convincing. It is led astray by man's deep-seated longing for nobility, idealism and self-sacrifice, without recognising the evidence of all that frustrates that longing – man's passion, despair, greed and self-seeking. 'European atheists, after the tragic experience of the suffering of Europe, often know better than Anglo-American humanism what is the size of the task confronting a movement which would replace the Christian vision of human destiny'. (D. Edwards, *op. cit.*)

The most widespread basis upon which various

attempts are made to define alternatives to theistic religion is that of evolutionary 'existentialism'. There are two main schools of thought associated with this term, and it is important to distinguish them and to know which of them we mean when we speak of existentialism.

The existentialism of Jean-Paul Sartre and Camus believes that natural evolution is the arbiter of human destiny – that truth, philosophical and ethical, is to be defined and redefined as evolution unfolds. There are no absolutes, and no 'basics'. All is subject to change.

The existentialism of Kierkegaard assumes certain basic hypotheses which are to be verified or falsified by one's experience of 'existence', including one's awareness of the evolutionary principle. Kierkegaard assumes the sanctity of human personality and the existence of a divinity behind the universe, and in experience and one's interpretation of experience believes that those principles can be existentially verified.

Whatever may be said in favour of evolutionary ethics, there remains a profound discrepancy between what *is* and what *ought to be.* 'It is impossible to be sure that the evolutionary process ('is') does, in fact, encourage all forms of ethical behaviour which we admire ('ought')'. (D. Edwards, *op. cit*).

Although 'right' may be conditioned by an implanted group-urge for survival, there is much unaccounted for by this thesis. For example, acts of self-sacrifice which are ethically honoured may be the exact opposite of the urge to survive, and many

39

ethical decisions are made in the commonplaces of life, such as honesty in business and industry, which have no relation to survival and could cost the honest man his livelihood. 'Natural selection is amoral, and so cannot have produced a man's moral or spiritual characteristics'. (D. Lack, *Evolutionary Theory and Christian Belief: the Unresolved Conflict.*) Without a religious faith, much of man's moral and spiritual behaviour makes no sense whatever.

The evolutionary process is magnificent, but it has no divinity within it. If human nature continues to want an object at all like the God of traditional religion, then evolution as the object of worship will not give an emotional assurance at all like traditional religion at its best.

Philosophy objects that no amount of scientific facts on their own, arranged by the theory of evolution, can produce a system of ethical imperatives, nor arouse worship; perhaps wonder and fear, but not worship, and certainly no clear conception of right and wrong.

The inconsistencies of the evolutionary humanists become clear when they are under pressure to explain what, within the science of evolution, is inexplicable. Julian Huxley (*Essays of a Humanist*) writes: 'In place of eternity we shall have to think of enduring process; in place of salvation, in terms of attaining the satisfying states of inner being which combine energy and peace. There will be no room for petitionary prayer, but much value in prayer involving aspiration and self-explanation'. Attempting to expand the definition of these Christian truths – eternity, salvation and prayer – does not offer an honest denial of their compelling intuitiveness in human experience. H.G. Wells was bereft, in his old age, of any help, when he felt a deep need for it, from the evolutionary philosophy he had earlier propagated.

Teilhard de Chardin (*The Phenomenon of Man*) refuses to accept the common assumption of an antithesis between evolutionary science and religion. A study of science without a prejudice against religion must, in his view, lead to an awareness of the validity of the area of concern which has occupied the thought of men of religion. A study of religion without a mind closed to the insights of science must, in his view, lead to an acknowledgement of the evidence of God the Creator at work in natural evolution, and not to stubborn dependence on non-scientific mysticism as a defence against the insights of science.

To Teilhard, the way to an understanding of God is through an understanding of man who was made 'in the image of God'. He writes (*op. cit.,* p.283): 'If there is a future for mankind, it can only be imagined in terms of a harmonious conciliation of what is free with what is levelled up and totalised. All the signs and all our needs converge in the same direction and we need, and are irresistibly being led to create, by means of and beyond all physics, all biology, all psychology, a science of human energetics'. It is in the course of that creation, already obscurely begun, that science, being led to concentrate on man, will find itself increasingly face to face with religion.

Evolutionary science without religion, therefore, is

41

a means without an end. Religion without an acknowledgement of its need for the verification which science can provide is too often an arrogant assertion of an end in itself.

So much for a very cursory attention to scientific evolution as an attempted substitute for theistic and ethical religion.

Next, there are those who search in nature for a substitute for God; who 'seek to meet the needs of human nature's surviving religious sense within the categories of secularism'.

The religious value of nature may be mediated through natural science. The scientific method of searching for true definitions of the observable universe provides an array of valuable analogies of the religious interpretation of truth. The greatest danger to human life, if not to the existence of the physical universe, lies precisely, however, in the fact that the physical power of natural forces lacks the moral power to affirm and to secure their proper use. Hiroshima and Nagasaki bear witness to this; air pollution and the careless disturbance of the ecology of nature verify our fear of scientific advance undisciplined by a wide moral awareness of its consequences. The passions to which people are subject will not be tamed by making them pure intellectuals or competent scientists or efficient industrialists. It has always been the primary role of religion to provide the moral insights and discipline necessary to tame them. The religious claim that these moral insights are objectively secured in a divine and absolute moral imperative is not weakened by

42

any evidence of the success of empirical or 'situation ethics' in restraining man's natural passion for greed, cruelty and selfishness.

For some it is in the benefit of scientific-technological achievements that a substitute for religion is to be found. The 'space race' is the ultimate of these achievements. In the face of the growing gap between rich and the poor, the powerful and the weak, the confident and the despairing, 'we may suspect that even in this age of triumphant technology not many manage to sustain a devotion to applied science as the central enthusiasm of a lifetime' (David Edwards, *Religion and Change* p.245). Technology is valued because it delivers the goods to feed and heal and comfort people; 'but many fear that technology, if worshipped by itself, would produce a waist-high culture' (*ibid.*).

Others, in their search for a religion in nature find satisfaction in nature interpreted in art and 'culture'. The spread of popular publications, the increase of interest in art, the growing dependence on television, the multitudes of tourist nomads, all bear witness to the reality of art and culture as a possible substitute for religion. This is not to be regarded cynically, especially in the rediscovery of music made possible by the ease with which everyone can have access through gramophone records to great musical works. 'Through music the deep emotions of joy, triumph, suffering, loneliness, love, peace can be made articulate. The art of man can interpret the world, can console and celebrate; and this is for many an effective substitute, neither self-conscious nor artificial, for the ceremonies and atmosphere of the old religion' (D. Edwards, *op. cit.*).

The Bible itself provides the most complete confirmation of all these truths – the 'religion' to be identified in nature, in man's achievement, in art. The fact that man's achievements have found high peaks of expression in the magnificence of medieval cathedrals, in the greatest expressions of the graphic arts, and superbly in some of the most beautiful music ever composed or performed, testifies to the religious validity of the insights into truth and the high emotions evoked by the natural world. It is not enough to protest that this response is purely aesthetic, for it is impossible to define the limits of the aesthetic, separating it from the religious aspirations which such an aesthetic response provokes.

Incidentally, it is worth noting that the debasement of art by religion is more than balanced by the debasement of religion by traditional art. Many of the theological problems which perplex the modern Christian are caused by artists' insistence through the ages on making 'images' of God. The result has been that we have lost the awe and wonder with which Old Testament man regarded God, whose very name could not be mentioned, far less his form depicted. Centuries of Christian art have so anthropomorphised God that it is a tenable hypothesis that Christ – the human Christ of Bethlehem, Capernaum or Calvary – has 'got in the way' of the inconceivable, transcendent God, the Yahweh of the ancient Hebrews, to whom Christ leads us as Mediator.

In the same way the dramatic arts, for all their

striving, are consistently failing to do comprehensively what traditional religion has done – the integration of the whole man in a whole society. 'Self-expression', uninhibited self-analysis and introspection may be valid objectives of what is called 'creative drama', if one's view of religion is purely evolutionary. Religion objects that it is redeemed man, and not unredeemed man, whom one longs to see realised, and here the much despised objective 'religious plays of the past', for all their *naïveté* pursued this objective with the achievement to their credit of many generations of informed Christian people.

Plays aimed merely at the 'self-projection' of the actors, with a secondary concern for the enlightenment of the audience, may be fulfilling for the actors taking part. Some have now gone to the length of pursuing the evolutionary theory to the point of uninhibited nudity in the course of their presentation, a practice not unknown in the pagan dances of primitive society. The Christian critic objects that while such plays may be revealing of the human predicament, they say little of the Christian hope of redemption or of the undeflected initiative of the grace of God.

Modern pressures on traditional life and values have evoked in the Christian Church a search for a new spiritual-cultural environment. This has led to a new and still-to-be-worked-out re-focusing on the Gospel, not contradicting, but yet discontinuous with the Church's past, and calling for a reinterpretation of doctrine that will satisfy neither fundamentalist nor

45

modernist. To quote Fr. Joseph Whelen S.J., 'It is necessary in this search, to beware of the pitfalls of Paul Tillich's existentialist questioning of the Gospels, where culture sets limits to the questions that may be asked, and thus restricts the answers of revelation. It is the perennial duty of Christian theology to show the inner coherence and self-identity, as well as the revolutionary character, of the 'faith community' through history. The effort to 'relate' is then shown to be what it is, the refusal to relativise; and theology and spirituality thereby remain limitlessly to be enriched by culture, without becoming the handmaid of sociology'.

Basic to all our uncertainties today is the uncertainty about our understanding of God. It is to that theology in contemporary society that we must now turn in our search for the 'basic' upon which a new spirituality must be founded.

4

God – Dead or Alive?

A CHRISTIAN would have to be deaf or wilfully reluctant to hear if he had not felt cause to look deeply into his own ideas of God, and to see how far his belief in God could sustain his faith and guide his life in the face of the penetrating inquiry and criticism directed in these days to that belief.

In a sense – but only a limited sense – we can take comfort from the fact that this attack on belief in God is by no means new. Even the theory of 'God is dead' is not new. The proposition is made by Nietzsche in *Die Froliche Wissenschaft,* where a madman asserts that God is dead. Nietzsche was one of the many who have made the subject of belief in God the centre of high-level philosophical and theological discussion. But such a comfort is limited; for what do ordinary, sincere, thinking Christians know of these learned discussions? They have been encouraged by the very Church which has everything to gain by exposing them continuously to every opportunity to seek the truth, to have nothing to do with such matters. It is a sad reflection on the Church's lost opportunities in the past that it has so seldom encouraged an honest discussion with those who were regarded as heretical; that it has closed the debate in a stereotyped 'orthodoxy'. One wonders whether the Church was afraid lest its faith was too weak to stand the test of inquiry; or was the theologian's grasp of the faith not strong enough to answer the philosopher critic? If it is the truth that we seek – the truth being God – how is it that we have been so lacking in confidence that the Holy Spirit would guide us into all truth, that we have been traditionally hostile to criticism?

There has therefore been built up a sense of security, unexamined, seldom questioned, associated with the formal acts of worship within the walls of a church. The Christian was encouraged, by this view, to wrap himself in an unconditional and uncritical surrender to God's word – an attitude defined as 'fundamentalism'; or seek refuge in an individualistic devotion to Jesus – an attitude defined as 'pietism'.

Now the 'problem' of God has become the property of the world press and, by means of this and other mass communication channels, the questionable property of the 'man in the street'. Public theological debates are to be welcomed, but do more harm than good if those who take part in them do not know what they are talking about. The blame for this must lie with the inadequate content and technique of the Church's teaching work, both in theological training seminaries, in the schools and from the pulpit. In consequence of this inadequacy neither theologians nor clergy were in any way prepared for the sudden religious storm caused by the *Honest to God* or the

God is Dead controversies, and were in consequence not able to do very much to calm it.

These calls to re-examine our basic belief in God are calls to question the 'package' God that the Church has inherited and continues to teach. We can no longer rest on the security of assumptions about the accepted theism of our society. The theistic basis of our thought and behaviour must be rediscovered and restated before it will be accepted afresh by a critical age.

We have taught, and been taught, about God's Grace, God's Love, God's Purpose, God's Will. And our teaching and learning assumes too much that we live in a society in which the word 'God' has definite intellectual meaning. Generally, thinking at any level on theological subjects starts with the assumption of 'God'. 'God' becomes the peg on which we hang everything conceivable, everything inconceivable.

Christians believe that ultimately God is exactly that. But it has to be established in our observation of the sweep of human history, in the behaviour of peoples, and in our self-awareness. It does not become true merely by asserting it.

For many people 'God', in the dogmatic theological definition of him, is the very point at which their doubts and their questioning begin. But, nevertheless, we tend to go on asserting him, his existence, his nature, his purpose, and his will. The result is that there is no incentive to penetrate further than God – behind God, as it were. This is one of those statements which are easily misunderstood. It is not suggested that there is another God behind God. But it is suggested that behind the dogmatic assertion of God, in the theological sense, is a whole area of philosophical thinking which makes the concept of 'God' meaningful. The basic assumption of the religious view of life, which must today be clearly and urgently defined, is not the existence of God, but the acceptance of the religious understanding of the nature of the universe, which makes the existence of God a tenable hypothesis, which then, in history, in man's reading of his experience, and in man's consciousness of his own nature, can be verified. It is within this readiness to 'rediscover' God from the starting-point of basic axioms relating to the nature of the universe, to the voice of history, to the dialectic inherent in human society and in individual personality, that the current trend to return to study of the Old Testament is to be understood.

A great deal of philosophical and theological understanding must supplement our dogmatic assertions about the manner of Christ being the revelation of God. It is tenable argument that we have limited our understanding of the infinitude and the unknowability of the God of the great mysterious Universe by constricting our understanding of him too rigidly in the humanity of Jesus.

Jesus is called Advocate, Mediator, Propitiator, High Priest, and many more titles defining the purpose of his Incarnation as being to restore man to a right relationship *with God,*, the God of Abraham and Isaac and Jacob, the God who created the world, the God whose love protected his people through the turbulence of history. It is to that God that we pray 'through Jesus Christ our Lord'. I must confess to a dislike of the tapestry in Coventry Cathedral which otherwise I have more reason than most to love. It suggests that the 'end' of our striving to know, the 'end' of our worship, is a Christ set in an almost mathematically definable frame, an end in himself, rather than one who goes to the Father, that where he is we might be also.

The 'God is dead' cry is a call to theologians to question the 'package', anthropomorphic God, and to devote more attention to the reluctance and awe with which the Old Testament writers spoke of God. Reverence prompted them to avoid even using his name, as far as this is possible. 'Yahweh' was not for them the name of an objective Supreme Being, but a form of address. God did not disclose his objective being, but revealed himself in the history of a people.

It is this divine revelation, especially at the present historic period of rapidation and change, which opens up a new perspective of history, and in consequence a new perspective of our personal 'self-consciousness' in relation to our present phase of history, that the 'death of God' theologians are anxious to emphasise. They are convinced that the mythical, objectively defined, 'religious' God must die before we can once again be open to the real revelation of God.

There are by now those who, having read these sentences, are ready to shoot the argument to pieces by firing selected texts at it. They could be attacked by a barrage of texts in return. Such is the familiar game of extracting texts from the coherent historical context within which they were first written. All too often this is what our attempt at theological debate looks like – playing games with words and images, while the world dialogue passes us by. And we must soon stop playing these games, for it is being said that the *real* questions – questions about the nature of things, and reasons for existence, questions about the nature of man, about the basis of moral authority, are being asked by mathematicians and physicists, technologists and sociologists, more clearly than they are by theologians. Those who ask these basic questions are seriously looking to the Church for help in examining them, but examining them honestly and not dishonestly, as so often happens when we slap a text or a dogma like a sticking plaster on a mouth asking a profound question.

Here are two such texts which are misused in this way. Set side by side they do not so much appear to cancel each other out as to highlight the theological predicament. The first is 'No man hath seen God at anytime'. The second is 'He that hath seen me hath seen the Father'. But there is a third which holds the secret of the theological understanding of God to which our present age beckons us: 'The Father who dwells in me does his work' – his work in history, in creation, in the search for truth, in human relationships.

The first of these texts, in full, is: 'No man hath seen God at anytime: the only begotten Son, he hath declared him.' 'Declared', not 'defined'. In the activity of God incarnate in the world, in creation, in history, in the nature and the genius of man, is the nature of God to be understood. It was the created world and man himself which Jesus came to enter, to affirm these as the 'laboratory' of God in action.

Belief in God is not an intellectual definition of God. 'Belief' in God is the acceptance of a framework within which one can enter into a living dialogue with the mystery of existence, of life, of suffering, of death, of good, of evil; a framework which contains more answers to the questions that are addressed to it than any other system of belief or conduct. If those who hold the Christian existentialist view of understanding God tend to overstate their case, it is simply because of the blind obscurantism of those who appear to believe that God has given no revelation of himself for 2000 years, that the Holy Spirit has not 'guided us into all truth' since the day that Jesus said he would.

Now to accept that God was 'declared' in the works of Jesus is to demand a clear understanding of what our attitude towards 'the world', in which Jesus declared God at work, really is. There is nothing ambiguous in the last commission of Jesus that we should 'go into all the world' and his promise that he would be with us. But we have given it a meaning which has safely liberated us from its more significant implications. It is easy to sentimentalise this commission in terms of 'Greenland's icy mountains and India's coral strand'; it is easy to sentimentalise it by a cheque to 'Christian Aid,' to 'Freedom from Hunger' or some other worthy cause. But our 'world' into which we are commanded to go to discern the works and try to understand the will of God for man, is no less the world of computers, of genetic studies, of technology, of physics, of industry, of urbanisation, of race, of processions of innocent victims of resurgent nationalism, of the world-wide undermining of moral standards. Have we made God too cosy and too remote to have any relevance to *this* world?

A major reason for the Church's failure to influence the direction of our world, and to direct moral principle in the corridors of power, is that she has sought refuge in the purely private sphere of life, and has come to feel safe and at home there. Religion has been 'privatised' and come to be regarded as the peculiar prerogative of certain people. The Church has become alienated from the creative and dynamic centres of society. In those very spheres in which man gives thought to, plans and realises his world and the world of the future, and his possibilities and those of the human race, the Church and her testimony have been absent.

This has not always been so. In the Middle Ages, Church and Society were to a large extent identical. False though that medieval synthesis ultimately was proved to be, at least the whole of life was seen to be the concern of God, and therefore the concern of the Church.

One of the reasons for the divorce of the Church from the mainstream of social progress was what, in some respects, has been the Church's greatest strength, namely the parochial system. It was a strength for the same reason that it will always be a strength, in that it demonstrated the love and concern of God for every individual in his home and his neighbourhood. It was a weakness because new structures of community have rapidly developed in our industrial age, and the Church has held on to the personal private relationship in the homes of its people, and had less and less ability to help and direct the same persons when, during the most active hours of the day, they were caught up by the great, relentless impersonalised industrial, commercial, political and technological monsters, which, none the less, have the power to direct events which affect the lives of everyone, whether they be in the private refuge of a parochial relationship in a church or not.

As Gibson Winter has said: 'A ministry to individuals and families in the context of residential association is no longer a ministry to society. In mass society, individuals contribute to decisions for the good or ill of the Society, but they make these contributions through the managerial hierarchies, labour unions, community organisations, political bodies, and bureaucratic units which organise their lives'.

Urbanisation has resulted in an ever-widening gulf between man's private life and his public work. The Church tends to concentrate on man's needs in the private sphere, and there is something gravely wrong with the Church's continued apparent withdrawal into this circumscribed and restricted sphere of life. The New Testament is rich in parables which define the Church's total identification of itself with the life

55

of the world which it was commissioned to redeem.

Let it be recalled that this chapter is concerned with the Christian and his understanding of God. Everything that is said about the Church in the world is a direct reflection of our ideas of God – whether he is the God of the Universe, still actively interested in his ongoing creation, or whether he is only the Jesus of the streets of Capernaum or the hillsides of Galilee 2000 years ago. If our understanding of God is inadequate and small, our Church and its witness will be inadequate and small.

It is undoubtedly true that 'the world' –,whatever that means – certainly the world represented by a great majority who are caught up in the direction of the world's affairs – *wants* God to be made relevant. It wants the Church to *be* the Church. People despise the Church when they see it is not the Church that they know it could be. They brush aside much of the Church's activity as being totally irrelevant, but they long for the Church to rise to the opportunity of today's crisis in human history, to reaffirm a belief in human destiny and to reaffirm a powerful moral discipline as a basis of social and national life. Too often the Church looks like the picture drawn of it by an East German Marxist, of 'people meeting behind stone walls to memorise the old phrases in order to make the absence of God in the world more bearable'. When the Church gets its understanding of God clear, and therefore also its theology of the Church, it will so structure itself and inform its members, that it will be able to demonstrate the *presence* of God in the world, rather than make his 'absence more bearable'.

This will require of Christians that they lose many of their treasured prejudices and become less resistant to new experiments; that they do a great deal more serious study in order to re-examine some of the old traditional images of God which have remained unchallenged since childhood; that they are not content with a faith so shallow that it wilts under the first breath of critical air from new scientific insights, or under some atheistic utterance of the reigning pop-singing 'king'.

In a residential environment, in which we have largely been content to limit the effective life of the Church, the most important activity is Sunday worship. Parishioners are encouraged to 'come to church', to 'join in the liturgy', but 'its largely outdated and mythological phraseology makes real understanding of the liturgy almost impossible.· Preachers readily lapse into pseudo-religious sentimentality, tend to moralise and exhort, or emphasise the need to encourage the growth of the purely personal spiritual life' (Adolfs, *The Grave of God*).

The objection to this is not that it is wrong, but that it is inadequate; that we are not really getting to grips with our theological study in such a way that we *know* why moral standards in politics and business are possible; that we *know* the danger points at which automation can dehumanise our already largely impersonalised society; that we *know* that the concept of God is ultimately inconceivable in human intellectual terms, but that our daily experience of life makes

57

us aware of his reality through experience of a dimension of life which is higher than physical; that we *know* that knowledge is more than can be fed into a computer.

Bishop Lesslie Newbigin (*Honest Religion for Secular Man*) writes well of the wider dimension of knowledge particularly in relation to our knowledge of God. The Christian must affirm categorically that knowledge is more than can be fed into a computer. The Bible has its own profound definition of knowledge which relates to a 'level of personal, mutual recognition, a relationship of persons, even at times to the extent of referring to the act of intercourse between a man and a woman in love as being the ultimate of knowledge'. In this sense Adam *knew* his wife Eve. Knowledge is the 'total mutual self-revelation and surrender of persons to one another in love', the supreme operation of *persons*.

It is this Biblical understanding that defines the knowledge of God. It is a category of knowledge which involves perseverance in the skill of knowledge – progress in learning to know.

Knowledge does not impose itself upon us. It is acquired by being learned, by gaining the will and the skill necessary for carrying out the mental operations involved in learning. All progress in knowledge depends upon the existence of a community of persons who share their experience and who mutually trust one another to accept a certain basic framework of inquiry. This is essentially why the community of the Church is necessary. Its members accept certain standards of human fallibility, as well as the infinity of truth into which, by steps marked by an honest study of history and experience, we grow.

Knowledge of any sort involves a risk and a commitment. By searching for knowledge in a community of people who acknowledge the risk, one can accept certain beliefs which might be mistaken, but which are asserted as acts of faith on the understanding that they can be verified or falsified, both by human experience and philosophical insights. Science, for instance, has not advanced by the method of sticking to facts which cannot be contradicted, but quite the opposite.

It is strange that so many scientists try to suppress this obvious fact, and to suggest that scientific theories are simply imposed upon the mind of the scientist by facts which cannot be disputed. Scientific knowledge advances by taking the deliberate risk of making propositions in advance of accepted knowledge, and embarking on an experiment to verify or falsify those propositions.

Religious knowledge has advanced in the same way; by making propositions experimentally in advance of accepted theological beliefs, and if necessary embracing 'heresy' experimentally, even if only to retreat into 'orthodoxy', having verified its truth. It is just as possible to be led astray by too much faith as it is by too much doubt.

Religious knowledge has advanced by believing in order to understand, by defining and continually verifying the basics of belief – about the nature of existence, about man, about God – in order to understand the emergence of new categories of what

59

suggest themselves as basics in the constantly changing areas of the variables.

Religious knowledge, in particular knowledge of God, will be constricted and impoverished if it assumes that there may be no areas of doubt, that knowledge of God must necessarily be knowledge which is proof against doubt. One begins with a basic proposition, then one must verify it through the living experience of one's self and in company with others.

The current fashion to define God, or the nature of the metaphysical area in which God exists, makes dialogue with those whose discipline compels them to use language which has definite meaning more and not less difficult. The fashion adds nothing to the method of accepting 'God' as a hypothesis which is capable of being verified by our experience of wrestling with the ultimate mystery of 'Why does anything exist?', capable of being verified, further- more, by our experience of love, by the common experience of the need for justice, mercy, truth, forgiveness, honour and moral integrity. The non- believer makes no progress if he eliminates 'God' as a tenable hypothesis and then uses language about human experience which has no meaning apart from a personal God, whose attributes are identifiable in the very experiences through which we can comprehend him.

Here is a quotation relevant to the theme of this chapter. It comes from the *The Modern Predicament* lectures by H.J. Paton.

'In our time there is a special need for intellectual

honesty. Religious teachers must be humble enough
to face intellectual difficulties and to admit how little
they know. A revival of religion will never come by
mere thinking, not even by religious thinking; but,
without a supreme effort of thought which will
satisfy the mind as well as the heart, religion will not
easily recover its former influence or restore to men
the spiritual wholeness which many of them prize but
seek in vain.'

The predicament caused by the gulf between faith
and knowledge is acute in the modern world, but it is
also very old. Here are some words from Plato,
writing three and a half centuries before the birth of
Christ. In his dialogue called the *Phaedo* he puts these
words into the mouth of Simmias:

'I think, Socrates, as perhaps you do yourself, that
about such matters it is either impossible or
supremely difficult to acquire clear knowledge in our
present life. Yet it is cowardly not to test in every
way what we are told about them or to give up before
we are worn out with studying them from every point
of view. For we ought to do one of the following
things; either we should learn the truth for ourselves;
or, if this is impossible, we should take what is at
least the best human account of them, the one
hardest to disprove, and sailing on it, as on a raft, we
should voyage through life in the face of risks –
unless one might be able on some stouter vessel,
some divine account, to make the journey with more
assurance and with fewer perils'.

The persevering Christian has the advantage of
both alternatives mentioned by Simmias. The raft on

which we sail through life in the face of risks is both 'the best human account of them, the one hardest to disprove', because we can interpret our human experience of Jesus; and it is also 'some divine account', a 'stouter vessel', because God was in Christ, and by the lives of his followers through history, 'reconciling the world unto himself'.

5

Perspectives of the Church in a Changing World

IT IS fashionable to give titles to the Church today which may express contempt, cynicism, despair or confidence and hope. We do well to take this seriously. Even a title of contempt contains an element of truth, to face which, with humility, could give us the will to right the wrongs and strengthen the weaknesses of the Church.

The title *The Grave of God* was chosen as a 'sequel' to the title *God is Dead.* Its cynicism is directed by the author of the book of that title mainly to the Roman Catholic Church during its retreat into conservatism following the enlightened era of Pope John XXIII. But the main categories of the bitter cynicism which the book contains are accurately applicable to every Church.

When the Church is called 'post-Constantine' it is a reminder of the long period during which the Church had been protected by the State, and in many nations continues to be. The taking over by the State, however, of many social services which the Church had, to its credit, faithfully provided for centuries, has led to the healthy situation in which the Church is compelled to ask of itself what precisely it exists for.

A helpful picture of the Christian today is that of a modern good Samaritan who stands side by side with a fellow human being, beaten up on one of the countless modern roads from Jerusalem to Jericho, and looking at him, realises that he has no oil, no wine, no beast, not a penny piece and nothing to give but himself. It is then, as G. Studdert Kennedy said in a sermon on the subject, that a man asks 'What am I worth?'; and he cries to God for help.

Separated from all the largesse which, in past centuries, the Church has been able to distribute, in terms of leadership in education, care of the vagrant and the sick, the Church now finds itself in the position of being able to define precisely, and in meaningful theological terms, what it exists for.

The Church is also referred to as *Una Sancta* — One and Holy — a 'sacred brotherhood', a Holy Fellowship. Whatever the human failings of the Church, and however frustrating its anachronistic divisions, that remains the ideal to which Christians must aim.

This places a direct responsibility upon clergy and ministers. Any jealousy and division among those who are chosen and ordained to lead the Christian Church is a betrayal of the love and forgiveness of the Lord Christ. If love is, as Jesus insisted, the essential mark of discipleship, then that love must be most evident among those who are called and ordained to be leaders of the loving community. *Invidia clericalis,* the jealousy of the clergy, is too common a reaction to the problems created for the Church in these complex days. Yet the common nature of the problems should provoke a more common love and a greater mutual dependence. The central danger to any Christian institution is that it may not have love at its heart.

It is, however, in the title 'Exodus Church' that the perspective of the Church are most helpfully defined. There are elements in the great biblical saga which are precisely relevant to situations over which we agonise in the 'exodus' era in which we are living.

The people of Israel had been in Egypt for four hundred and thirty years. That is about the length of time by which today we are separated from the Reformation. The saga of Israel in Egypt contains little of detail, but the picture of a people whose early tribal identity and cohesion had been broken by their integration into the social and economic system of Egypt is clear enough. The fragmentation of Church and Society in Europe since the Reformation needs no long description. For all its benefits, it offered no central loyalty to hold together the social, industrial, national, cultural as well as religious divisions which for five centuries have mocked Europe's hopes of peace and unity.

It is only comparatively recently that the Church has been conscious of the need to establish its identity, in all this confusion and fragmentation, as the people of God in the secular world. During the years of captivity in Egypt the Israelites had become

65

part of the whole social and economic system. They were the labouring class of a very class-ridden society. The Church today is no less enmeshed in the social and economic system of contemporary society of which it is a part. It is hedged about by the securities which the social system provides. It is secure in the financial structure of its endowments, safeguarded by the pledges of those who support it, but even more by its association with social respectability. 'Going to church' is a part of social behaviour, even though it may be less so than it was a generation ago. The identity of the Church is largely expressed in the long observance of customs, many of which have lost their original meaning with the passing of the years. During this time social behaviour has changed more rapidly than the traditional observances of Church practices.

Liturgical custom in particular, and scholastic mysticism, have maintained the thin line of tradition in much the same way as a little-understood liturgical custom held the thin line of identity in the case of the Israelites in Egypt. Even our buildings are dictated by custom. In them we go through the motions of the ancient rites and memorise the old words and phrases. Small wonder, then, that God has become for the multitude a vague idea and not a living reality. Small wonder that the Church has tended to become more and more irrelevant to the swiftly moving secular world.

At such times prophets are born. It is the role of a prophet to see the times in which he lives against the background of a perspective of history. He is able to discern the phases of history which have led to the situation in which he finds himself, the cumulative effect of forces in the past which have produced the contemporary situation. He is able to identify the basic needs of the present, be they moral, social, or political, in the meeting of which a people can renew themselves. So it was that Moses arose as the prophet of God. God's hand was upon him. His first clear objective was to reaffirm the identity of the Children of Israel as the people of God. And there is no greater need today than that the Church of God in the world should recover its identity — its ecumenical identity — as the people of God upon whom must rest the responsibility for renewing the hopes of humanity for the future.

Because Moses was alert to the possibility of being called by God, he was ready to respond when God met him in the course of his work — shepherding his father-in-law's sheep. Leadership in the Church, whether at a high level of professional leadership or at the level of moral leadership of ordinary Christian people, requires a measure of alertness to the moment of insight, and an ability to hold fast to the insight to the point at which it leads to action.

It is tempting to justify the existence of the Church solely by its efficiency and busy-ness. Yet that activity will lack clear purpose if it is not sustained by a prophetic vision of what can be achieved. There is a great need to *think* more; to get a prophet's view of the present and a prophet's perspective of the future.

On the whole, our church activities do not encourage this. The church services themselves tend to be filled with words, both spoken and sung, and never a moment must be left unfilled. There is a need to 'hush the spirit', to persevere in the discipline of silence. The busier we are in our daily work, the greater is the need to relax in silence, without feelings of guilt that we are *doing* nothing.

The growth of our cities and the speed of our motorways puts such intolerable pressure upon human emotions that it is less and less possible to make a calm judgment about events which happen around us. To use our churches and our church activities exclusively to talk, to sing, to listen to others talking compulsively, to discuss everything for the sake of discussing, is to deny ourselves one of the richest blessings of a church building and of the Christian view of living. Christian people could well be encouraged to use churches day by day merely to enter and sit in silence. Church administrators could encourage this by making them more comfortably conducive to this end. The proper concern to discern the will of God in the wind and the fire and the earthquakes of our contemporary tumultuous secular world must not deny us the experience of Elijah who found God's authentic presence in 'the sound of gentle stillness'.

Secondly, Moses responded to the call to prophecy by making use of his knowledge of the secular world. His upbringing had enabled him to find many points of entry into the corridors of power where policies and decisions were made.

The separation of secular life from religious life has largely inhibited Christian people from making use of their own knowledge of the points of entry into the corridors of secular power today as Christian people. Power is not a vague mystical influence. Power does not ultimately rest in people in an institutional or an abstract sense. Power resides in *persons*. It is always a person who at a high level, an intermediate level or a low level has the ability to say 'yes' or 'no' when any decision has to be made. It is always a person with conviction who can influence the making of a decision. There are many Christian people who in secular life have such power. To give effective response to their role as prophets it is necessary to bring to bear upon decision-making a passionate concern for justice, truth and integrity. We accept far too readily the cliché about the impossibility of being a Christian in commerce and industry. Far too little attention is drawn to the power of integrity based upon Christian principles in which a selfish or ruthless decision is outvoted because it is not honest. There is a more than usual need in our day for confidence that Christian morality *can* be applied to secular power. Without such confidence the Church has no right to complain if its witness in the corridors of power is slight.

Power is fragmented in our cities today among those who exercise specialist responsibility in the community. Members of the City Planning department, local politicians, bankers, industrialists, police, educators, and many more are all involved in decision-making. It is the task of the Christian Church to get alongside those who wield power. It is necessary to know them as persons, to make friends with them, to convey to them a passionate concern for coherence. In this way we could become the initiators of a creative dialogue between those who normally operate within their own specialisation and seldom communicate with other specialists.

Impersonal decision-making is too readily accepted by the general public without question. The 'infallibility' of bureaucratic authoritarianism too often makes a mockery of our claims to be upholders of democracy. The voice of protest against the increasingly arrogant and uncompassionate use of bureaucratic power is not heard as it should be heard. The Christian concern for justice for the voiceless citizen needs strong and persistent expression.

A third response of Moses to his call to prophecy was his courage. He was not dismayed by the 'moaners' among the Israelites. There is much 'moaning' in the Church today. There are many clergy and ministers who have begun to lose heart, and make no secret of their lack of faith. This pessimism soon communicates itself to congregations. It takes the form of persistent and negative criticism, with little affirmation of hope. It does not rejoice in the works of the Lord of history in the Church's witness in the past.

It leads the pessimists to give up saying their prayers, or to take refuge in 'being busy' to evade the burden of lost confidence in their faith. Organising bazaars, rummage sales, and social events are good subsidiaries but bad substitutes for effective Christian witness. Many clergy go through the motions of their professional occupation without any conviction. They are carried along by the momentum of the traditions of Church order and cultic ceremonies, without ever daring to step outside it to get an honest perspective of the challenge to renew their understanding of their faith, or being willing to undergo retraining in order to relate that renewed faith to the modern world's need for it.

There is, however, frequently a reason for pessimism among the clergy. There are many who wish to come to terms with their own honest inquiry into theology and the structure of the Church today. They find that their honest 'radicalism' (in the literal sense of the meaning of this word) isolates them from those who are content with a more conservative acceptance of theology in the Church (and these are in the majority), and they therefore feel themselves embittered and frustrated. There is a great need to form a warm fellowship of those who are critical, who have a desire to experiment, who are dissatisfied with the old wine-skins and long for new wine-skins into which to put their new wine. And the isolated radical tends to overstate his case in his frustration at not getting a hearing from the more 'established' minds.

'Moaning' is not a part of the Christian character. We are called to be men and women of faith and conviction. We are called to be people of initiative, to be salt in the meal and leaven in the dough. We are called to be high-minded and high-hearted enough to be able to recognise the germ of the future in the ground of the present. We are among those who are expected to batter down the walls of despair and

71

hopelessness and to build gateways into a future in which new visions can begin to take shape. The Church is called upon to rediscover its identity as a bastion of hope and optimism in a wilderness of despair and pessimism.

Following the Exodus analogy further, then, Moses led his people through the Red Sea. This was the moment of doubt. The subject of faith and doubt has been dealt with in a previous chapter. But in another sense Moses's call to 'stand still and see the salvation of our God' is too often reproduced in the Church as a readiness to 'consolidate', to 'play for safety', which takes the form of appointing a commission, asking for a report, forming a committee, calling a conference, or sometimes – instead of organising action – merely to have a service of intercession for a cause which is crying out for active Christian participation and the demonstration of courageous leadership.

This point in the Exodus saga is the point of true crisis. It was at this point that the migration might have ended, and there could have been a retreat into the safety of the old established situation. But at this point also the proper courage could have been summoned to go forward into the unknown. Migrations have marked formative points in human development. The creativeness is preceded by migration – a movement, an uprooting. So it has been throughout history, not only with the Israelites but with the Mongols, the Goths, the Celts, the Anglo-Saxons, the Spanish, the Europeans to America, the Europeans to Africa, a spread of European trade and culture. In all these, migration has been one of the preludes to new structures of society. And new problems are being posed today by movements of people – between nations, between races, within nations, between urban dwelling and suburban dwelling. In each case the same sort of crisis is being experienced. The decision is between holding on to the past indiscriminately and preserving what can be preserved as a safeguard against the hazards of change; or, on the other hand, holding on to the basic values of the past and going courageously into the unknown future.

The shift of population and the changes of community have undoubtedly made nonsense of many of the old patterns of church relationships to communities in which they have by tradition, been comfortably set. People travel by car from suburbia in search of the old patterns, to the parish churches of their fathers, which by now may be isolated churches in an industrial area, a commercial centre, an educational complex, a hospital area, or a negro 'ghetto'. And such churches remain inflexibly parish-centred in the old exclusively pastoral style, with evident and cynical irrelevance to the nature of the new community about them.

There is a great need to rationalise our strategic thinking and to be a little less imprisoned in the endowed structures of our financial investments which have safeguarded a disappearing past. We might then use the 'plant' of the churches which have been left behind by the departing residential communities to serve the needs of the new communities in the industrial, commercial and administrative centres,

73

rather than to serve the personal needs of an ecclesiastical club, whose members live their lives in a suburban community to which they escape from the very pressures which a related city church should be there to meet. A church in a ghetto could have a rummage sale to support itself and make thirty dollars, while a church in suburbia could have a rummage sale and make a hundred thousand dollars.

The maldistribution of the Church's wealth, and the failure to identify priorities to equip the Church with the courage to loosen its hold on the safe ecclesiastical-social structures of the past, are obstacles to the necessary will to launch out courageously into new areas of ministry, such as team ministries, ecumenical ministries, ministries to professional rather than residential communities, and so on.

The pursuing Egyptians create the dilemma. The Egyptians want Moses and the Israelites to return. They need the children of Israel. In exactly the same way the world is prepared to concede that it needs the Church. It is good for morality, it is good for children, it is good for our customs, it is good for deaths and marriages. Provided the Church is prepared to be accepted on the world's terms, the Church is always acceptable. But such a Church will lose all power to lead to a new future, for it will lose the courage which comes from the facing of danger and uncertainty.

God's call to Moses was quite unequivocal: 'Speak unto the children of Israel that they go forward'. Faith is taking the deliberate risk of trusting God. And so the Children of Israel went into the wilderness.

The future into which the Church is moving today is very much like a wilderness, and from this point on in the Exodus analogy there is much upon which to reflect.

The first task of Moses in the wilderness of Sinai was to re-establish the true identity of the Israelites as the people of God. And it was important that at the very beginning of the awareness of their identity the moral law should be incorporated in the Ten Commandments, and this was to be the basis of their national identity. It is at this point that there occurs one of the most dramatic texts in the Bible — 'Moses drew near unto the thick darkness where God was'. It is in the thick darkness of the problems of our day, the problems of urbanisation, of race, of man's scientific arrogance, of unresolved wars, of the bitter hatreds which have been bequeathed by unhealed wounds of the past; it is in the thick darkness of the moral anarchy of our day, and the despair and fear of the future, that we must know that the will of God is to be found. It is required of Christians who wish to respond to the call of God today, to be prophets. They must refuse to stand outside the 'thick clouds of darkness', and pontificate about them in an academic way. It was out of Moses, wrestling in the darkness to the point where he knew what he had seen, that he was able to present to the nation a strong moral code based on belief in God, a disciplined family life, and respect for fellow human beings.

It is time that the Church reaffirmed its allegiance to absolute moral values, and ended the sloppy opportunism which has led it to pay court to 'situation ethics' and sentimental humanism. If the Church does not know for what moral principles it stands, let it not be surprised if the secular world regards it with contempt.

A moral standard must be braced by a personal and corporate discipline. With the breakdown of the old traditional patterns of community has come a threat to, and a widespread questioning of, the framework of spiritual discipline as the Church has traditionally practised it. The search for a 'new spirituality' is the subject of a later chapter.

It is easy to speak of 'the Church', however, in a way which safely protects individual members of it from their duty at the local church level. The Church is not a vague idea. It is a fellowship of people who try to provide a local example, in advance, of that rich, loving fellowship of mutually respecting and mutually dependent people who are honestly searching for truth, for unity and for the quiet mind, which is the first gift of security at the deep level of love.

Let us now consider the role of the local church in our contemporary world.

6

The Role of the Local Church in the Twentieth-Century World

THIS is probably the most immediate question demanding an answer of Christian people in the world today.

Let us go back in history to trace the extent to which this is, or is not, a new problem. Go back to the Old Testament and we find that in the time of Moses there was no problem, because Moses thought of the people as totally the people of God. The 'Church' and the 'world' were one. The five Law books of the Old Testament not only laid down the specifically moral law, but also the law for 'secular' society – political, social and even for physical health.

Further on in the history of the Old Testament, one finds again the same synthesis, the same unity. In the time of Samuel, Saul and David the nation was the people of God. The figurehead of this unity was first Samuel the priest, then Saul and then David, the anointed ones.

A change is discernible in the post-Solomon era.

The wealth of the nation under Solomon gave a self-sufficiency to the 'secular' world, and a growing gulf appeared between those who spoke for God, as did Elijah and Elisha, on the one hand, and the secular, political power on the other. So by the time of the writing prophets, the secular and political had taken on a character which was so obviously at variance with the laws laid down by Moses, that the prophets felt themselves called upon bitterly to denounce the nation and to think in terms of an undefiled 'remnant' who 'had not bowed the knee' to pagan gods – which were the centres of the worship of essentially secular ideals. Here, then, we see the beginning of a withdrawn group which held to their loyalty to God, and made explicit certain beliefs, in opposition to the secular world.

There is a slight redress of this antithesis when we enter the centuries immediately before the coming of Christ. In the history recorded in the books of the Maccabees, Israelite nationalism, inspired by the God of their fathers, was as fierce and as purposeful as it had been in the days of Joshua. As in the days of David, the people of God were again identified with the national political aspirations.

And so, in this rather summary, and necessarily superficial, stride through history, we reach the time of Jesus. Again, religious observance became compromised with the fierce nationalism of the Jewish people in their opposition to the Roman conqueror. Much of the power of the Jewish worshipping community as represented by the High Priest and the Sanhedrin, was a political power. It was only as a political power that the Roman conquerors paid any attention to the Jewish religious leaders – as evidenced in the trial of Jesus.

In this situation Jesus seems to call out of the secular world a group of people to be 'chosen', to be an image of perfection. 'Come ye apart', 'I have chosen you out of this world', are examples of the sort of text one could quote – and there are many – to prove that Jesus intended the Church to be apart from the world. The very word 'Church' could be taken to confirm this exclusiveness if one accepts the assumption of opposition between the sacred and the secular. It derives from the Greek *kuriakon*, meaning, 'belonging to the Lord'. Those who reject, for today's mission to the world, the implications of this antithesis, 'belonging to the Lord' and 'belonging to the world', need to come to terms with another title for the Church – ekklesia – meaning 'called out'.

But against this stands arrayed a long list of the 'parables of the kingdom' – the salt salting the meal, the leaven leavening the dough, the light on a candle-stick, the net gathering every kind of fish, the lost sheep, and so on. It seems clear that those 'called', or 'belonging to the Lord', were not called for the luxury of being exclusive, but in order to enter the world to claim it for the kingdom. And before we regard this as supporting evidence for the view that the world is merely fair game for evangelism to bring over to the 'Church' side of the fence, let us ponder what Christ meant when he proclaimed to the crowd 'the kingdom of God is among you'. For who is not familiar with the dilemma of the good man or woman in society, who lives an impeccable life of honesty, justice and compassion, but who never 'goes to church'? It is this dilemma which demands an answer to the question, 'What, then, is the real contribution of the *ekklesia* to the world, if the world is able to produce perfectly good people without it?'

But for the moment, let us resume our perfunctory journey through history. Before we leave the time of Christ let us note that we see in his view of the relationship between 'Church' and the 'world' a relationship – a paradoxical relationship which differs from anything we have encountered in the Old Testament.

When we come to the Church of St. Paul, we see it was a persecuted Church, whose intense concern was to preserve its identity against a massive intention on the part of the 'world' to destroy it. The Pauline image of the Church is of small groups existing for themselves and for the eternal life which was thought to be about to replace the temporal life of the world. The eschatological urgency of much of Paul's preaching was to make perfect the 'called'. Paul wrote his letters not to people involved in the political and social life of the secular world of the Roman Empire, but to those having to hold on to their identity as members of the *kuriakon* against the pressures of the Roman secular world. It would be difficult to over-state the degree to which the doctrine of exclusiveness in Christian tradition has been influenced by the letters of St. Paul, and how different could have been the history of the Church if the truths of the salt and the leaven had not been so heavily obscured by the Pauline mentality of persecution, exclusiveness and passionate, though short-sighted, eschatological visions. It is when the Church looks most like an ecclesiastical 'ghetto' that we find ourselves turning to Paul's teaching of salvation and justification when we should be hearing the ringing tones of the Mount of the Ascension, 'Go ye into all the world'.

But on again. We are in the fourth century, when the Emperor Constantine made Christianity respectable and 'established'. There are many who regard this as being the beginning of the downfall of the Christian faith as a formative instrument in the perfection of human society. This is a view which must be held with reservation. Historically, bearing in mind the Christian basis of much in our civilisation which we now take for granted, it is possible to argue the opposite.

And again in our sweep through history, we enter the Dark Ages, when the Constantinian society collapsed. One of the most glorious periods in European history followed these centuries of destruction and gloom, namely the revival of the monastic movement, and in particular, the Benedictine Order. Great centres were established to demonstrate the concern of the Christian Church for the whole of society and not merely for a 'religious' part of it. Each centre had communication with every other centre in the network of monasteries throughout Britain and Europe.

The Benedictines did not see religion as one little circle among many other little circles – political,

81

economic, social, educational and the rest. To them religion is the great circle that can be drawn around the whole of life. It was a partial return to the Mosaic view of wholeness which inspired their outlook and activity, though without the political advantages of either the Mosaic or the Constantinian system.

All good ideas are liable to be corrupted, and so it was with the monastic vision, which saved Europe for two centuries after the Dark Ages. The return to the hope of a Holy Roman Empire found ready theological rationalisation in medieval Europe. The forcing of the whole of life, scientific, political, cultural, and social into a theological synthesis gained for the Church great political power, but sowed the seeds for centuries, of difficulty in the waves of reaction against such a synthesis, the effects of which reaction we are experiencing today in the sustained criticism of, and active opposition to, the institutional Church.

The Emergence of the modern Church-World Division

The attack on the medieval synthesis, which assumed that religious, political and social traditions are held together in a coherent cultural tradition, began with the Renaissance, and has continued to the present day. The *Aufklärung,* or Enlightenment, of the last century represented the climax of the secularisation of the European tradition. The political revolution produced the *Rights of Man*. The cultural revolution produced the emancipation of thought, and had as a consequence an implication of the bank-

82

ruptcy of Christianity. The scientific revolution appeared at the time to undermine the basis of a religious view of existence. New techniques of thought thought and expression took the place of the old dogmatic authoritarianism. In Germany in particular, the eighteenth and nineteenth centuries were centuries of poetry rather than prose, and explored in experimental outline the shape of a new world of thought.

While, at first, rationalism appeared to make the divorce between religion and culture complete, yet religion and culture were merely more clearly distinguished, and the definitions of each more clearly established. The very fact of their being so distinguished made possible a new relationship between them. Neither religion nor culture, nor any supposed synthesis between them were taken for granted, or assumed to be imposed by tradition, but were arrived at personally and freely.

The revolt against the medieval synthesis during the nineteenth century took two main forms; the one was the form of idealism, and the other the form of positivism. The proper understanding of the main direction of this revolt against a tradition which had become an inseparable part of the life, teaching and power of the institutional Church, is important in order to understand the nature of the dilemma implicit in the question of the relevance of the Church to our contemporary secular world at the local or at the national levels.

The idealistic revolt was exemplified largely in the secular philosophers. It was the age of Hegel and

Kant; its musical expression was Beethoven's Ninth Symphony. The philosophy of religion took forms which did violence to traditional dogmas. Given modern means of communication the philosophical revolt against traditional dogmas would have popularised the 'God is dead' theology a century ago, for it was implicit in Schleiermacher, Troeltsch, Feuerbach, Freud, and Nietzsche, among others.

The positivist revolt found its clearest expression in Karl Marx and Friedrich Engels. The secular world was the only realistic area of study. The only valid philosophy was political, economic and social. The positivists were nurtured in the cradle of the Industrial Revolution. The failure of the Church to nurture a new mission for the Christian faith in the same cradle led to the separation of the Church from industrial society, which, more than anything else, has led to pertinent questions being asked about the irrelevance of the Church to the contemporary world. This failure has not yet been noticeably redeemed by any evident determination on the part of the Church today to bridge the gap between itself and the man engaged in industry.

At the time of the Industrial Revolution Europe and Britain were essentially rural. The local church was in an effective sense the centre of the whole community, and the source of educational, social and cultural activity. The vast sprawl of industrial cities followed in less than a century and the momentum of their growth continues unabated. It is a commonplace of history that the Church made no attempt whatsoever to consider, to define and then to relate to this

84

other unit of community — the industrial area, with all its specifically industrial and social problems. It continued blindly to believe that the parish or local congregation is the only recognised 'community'. At that time the Church lost touch with the working man, and it has never effectively regained it. Let it be clearly understood, therefore, that the Church has to start its mission of relevance to the modern industrialised society virtually at 'square one', and let no member of the local church either ignore this other dimension of the Church's mission, or claim that there is any easy answer to the question of our relevance in relation to that mission.

The secular world has plenty to be getting on with. It has political problems which demand a profound examination of the basics of democracy itself. It has industrial problems which, at least in Britain, stem more from emotions from a long-departed past than from any rational appreciation of industry's perils in the present. Racial problems are no longer remote from the local scene as in the days of a colonial empire, but an agonising part of it. Migration of populations is not concerned with national migrations or colonisation projects, but with movements of rural populations to swell the gigantic urbanisation problems which grow with unabated complexity.

The solution of these problems demands an agreement on the part of all who wrestle with them that the heat of emotion, prejudice, fear, greed, pride must be taken out of them, and the clear light of basic religious and moral values be reasserted — values of truth, compassion, justice, understanding of the value of the human personality – the principles around which alone a community can be composed in any permanent sense. All these and many more are to be found in the Christian Faith, even if the ponderous obscurantism of the institutional Church often obscures them. Our modern secular society at its best is the product of centuries of patient Christian witness. But we cannot rest on the achievements of the past, and be content to remain ineffective in relating to the problems of the present.

Nor can any but the bitterest cynic say that we invariably do. The local church and the individual Christian can take heart from the incredible amount of good done in our wounded world by the initiative of Christian people. Where the local church provides a leadership which relates to real needs, and to needs which can be met by personal involvement, the results are apparent and considerable. When, however, the church relies only on remote control techniques, like having a rummage sale for a hospital in Thailand, about which no parishioner knows a thing, the vision fades and the fire goes out.

An Analogy of the Role of the Church

I want to expand this by extending an analogy. A modern motorway is a good image of life in the 'secular' world. Speed, beating the man in front, urgency to get to a destination, aggressive behaviour at the wheel, impatience with others, fear of the unpredictable behaviour of others, fragile, yet implicitly trusting, dependence on the technological

age as represented by the motor car one is driving —
all these being slightly balanced by the tolerance,
good manners and concern for others on the part of a
minority. It is not altogether fanciful to see this as a
small image of the main characteristics of
twentieth-century life, which imposes upon human
beings the pressures under which most suffer.

And from time to time in the journey down the
motorway, one reaches a service area, or motel, or
refreshment park, with seductive invitations to draw
aside from the motorway for one or other of the
services provided. The analogy I want to press a little
will identify the motorway with the pressures and
stress and aggressiveness of the 'rat-race', and the
service area — for the purpose of the theme of this
chapter — with the Church, particularly the local
church.

The first thing one notices on drawing into a
service area and entering the restaurant is that
everyone else there looks as tired and strained as one
feels oneself. There is a common level of communication based on the common factor of need. The size,
cost or power of the motor car of each traveller, their
evident wealth or poverty, their place of origin or
destination — all this becomes entirely irrelevant to
the common factor of each being tired, hungry, and
needing to relax.

So it should be with the local church or congregation. Its character must be recognised first by those
who belong to it, as being the character of a common
need. It is not necessary to labour the point as to
what that need is. It is the need for the security of

87

love and trust. It is in this context of *the* basic need of human society that Christ's definition of the characteristic of the belonging community is to be understood. 'By this shall all men know that ye are my disciples: if ye have love one for another.' Such phrases have become so familiar that listeners 'switch off' when they hear them. But this is because we too often *speak of love* without identifying the *need for love* in our life together in the secular community. It is in this context of the need for love and trust that we really are to believe that the local Christian congregation is capable of being an image of a coherent community within an incoherent society. The restaurant in the service area off the motorway often has, momentarily, a real and profound sense of fellowship, because there is recognition of a common need.

Christian congregations fail when the meeting, the liturgical service, the decoration of the buildings or the management committee which directs it, become ends in themselves. But when these things are seen and felt to relate to an evident and common need, they immediately come alive. Only when an honest assessment of the needs of those who meet is made, can what is done honestly contribute to a sense of community in meeting those needs. One of the weaknesses of the Church now is its firm establishment on the foundation of the middle class, one of whose characteristics is often to pretend that it has no needs. It is thought to be a weakness to confess to any need. The services of the Church glide comfortably over the necessity to identify any need that is common to all. It may well be that the greatest need of our society today is the security of trust and love, the acknowledgement of our extreme frailty under the emotional pressures alone. This is the deep need of the old, of the unwanted immigrant, and fundamentally of the young; but it is also the unacknowledged need of the middle classes. The Church is in a special position, by the definition of its special character, defined by Christ, to offer a relationship within which the weak can be strengthened by holding hands with the weak, to whom they are not afraid to be honest about their weakness. Only at that point can love begin to operate, for love involves the sincere and honest acknowledgement of need, accompanied by the readiness to fulfil it.

Among the great 'success stories' of the Church are the stories of the great parish priests of the East end of London in the 'bad old days'. There was a profound honesty in acknowledging need, and a profound love in meeting it. No one had to pretend to be what he was not; so Christ could, through his Church, gain access to people *as they were,* and not be prevented from gaining access to them because they were pretending they were not what they were. The needs of our middle-class society are different. But they are greater. The role of the local church is, first, to identify need, and then to create a fellowship to meet it. Peace of mind, trust, love, wisdom in guiding children through the rapids of contemporary history — these are primary needs. None can honestly say that the local church always makes them priority concerns.

It is no use pretending that all this is provided for by the mystique of the Holy Communion, or by meetings for prayer. These can be blasphemous if they do not express a living fellowship which is lifted to God as a 'living sacrifice'. The sacrifice does not create the living fellowship. It is intended that it should consecrate something that already exists.

The needs of 'the world', then, are real needs, as real as the needs of the motorist on the motorway; and they must be realistically met. In every age of similar crises, there has always been an element in the Church which has withdrawn into pietism. The passionate pietism which has punctuated the last four centuries of European Christianity can be understood accurately as a reaction against specific periods of assertiveness in the secular world. It is no accident that the period of greatest industrial, political and social upheaval in Europe in the first half of the nineteenth century was also the period in which most of our pietistic hymns were composed. Religion was personalised and 'privatised', and lost its authority to speak to national or cosmic issues. And the stronghold of this withdrawn pietism was in the exclusiveness of the local church congregations.

A second reaction against such times of crisis and pressure is the assertion of tradition, and its valuation for its own sake. Before the age of the motorway, the refreshment place, or even the filling-station, there was probably a picturesque wayside inn, or a thatched house, possibly once the local smithy, since converted into a filling-station. Wayside inns continue to exist on the byways, and they attract tourists whose main interest is historic or artistic. But they have no relevance to the thundering traffic of the motorway. It is easy to translate the image of this analogy into a similar situation in the Church. The picturesque village church, the Gothic or neo-Gothic town church, together with the antiquated administrative structure of the Church, have precisely the same irrelevance to the 'thundering traffic' of the twentieth-century secular world.

The second service provided by the service area on the motorway is food and physical refreshment. G. Studdert Kennedy once preached a sermon on the twenty-third psalm. Having painted a beautiful picture of the sheep grazing in beautiful pastures, beside a still, silent pool with the sky reflected in its heart, he then went out to demolish the picture he had just painted.

> It is not for the green and gold of summer fields that the sheep seeks to find them, but because they are good to eat. It is not for the sleeping beauty in the heart of the silent waters that the flock follows on to find them, but because they are good to drink. It is not luxuries that they ask of the shepherd, it is the bare necessities.

The Church in the nation or in the world will never be seen to be attempting to provide for the 'bare necessities' of an intellectually, emotionally and spiritually hungry people, unless it is first seen to be attempting to provide for the bare necessities of the local community. Thousands of pounds spent on luxuries to beautify a city church cannot provide for the 'bare necessity' of a community-centre where people can meet one another, and loneliness, cynicism or bitterness can be healed.

The first and most sustained task of any local church congregation is to study with meticulous care the neighbourhood within which it is set, and to try to identify an essential amenity which it lacks. It may be a play-centre for pre-school children or children on holiday. It may be a centre of meeting for teenagers who are bored with the lack of anything to do, because the town planners have forgotten them in their preoccupation with a new road system or multi-storey car parks, or with the high rising skyline of the city (a new version of current civic 'keeping up with the Joneses'). It may be taking a leading part in providing play facilities for children by fighting a civic battle for a play-street or a play-park. It may be, if it is that sort of community, providing a club where professional people can meet to consider the common ground which exists between the economist and the moralist, the town planner and the sociologist, the physicist and the historian.

Probably the most urgent need of the twentieth century is for a horizontal structure of communication between these vertical 'towers of Babel', in our universities, in our cities and in the centres of national policy-making. No effective structure exists at the local level for such a horizontal conversation. The Church's commitment to coherence and wholeness could give it an accepted authority to provide the amenities to achieve that wholeness, at least experimentally, at the local level. But the identification of need must be the identification of real need. There are many examples of false communication efforts by the setting up of study groups, for instance between parsons and doctors, which aim at forcing a scientific concern into a half-understood spiritual frame; and inevitably these are short-lived, and make any subsequent attempt at true dialogue more difficult.

Thirdly, the service area of the motorway enables one to fill the car with petrol — to provide the power to continue the journey; or, to apply the analogy, to point to the role of the local church as the centre of inspiration and hope. To quote van den Heuvel, the Church should be a 'clinic for public optimism'. We have come near to becoming a generation of 'moaners', and this is reflected at every level. If the local church 'Wayside Pulpit' could call a halt to its preaching of gloom or doom and its unrealistic 'come-and-meet-Jesus' messages, and simply list the things locally in any week or month for which the community can smile and feel thankful, it would be fulfilling the purpose of God more effectively than usually it does.

In terms of the 'rapidation' analogy of Adolfs in a previous chapter, there are many signs, politically, socially, in religion, in the behaviour of young people and in our bewilderment over the problems of race, that man is losing his nerve, and does not know which is the safe course to take between the rocks and whirlpools. Where that sort of leadership is provided in the dialogue and enterprises of a local Christian community the leadership is recognised and followed.

Where the Church appears, in terms of this analogy to be trying to fasten on to a rock, to avoid moving down the rapids to the new river, it is overwhelmed by the flood, and of no further use in providing a course that others can follow, and it could easily cease to exist by the time society enters the new period of history.

7

In Search of a Basic Spirituality

LITURGY, at its best, has always expressed the living community of those who performed it. A picture of the early Christian community is described in the second chapter of the Acts of the Apostles. 'They met constantly to hear the apostles teach, and to share the common life, to break bread and to pray. All whose faith had drawn them together held everything in common, with one mind they kept up their daily attendance at the temple, and, breaking bread in private houses, shared their meals with unaffected joy, as they praised God and enjoyed the favour of the whole people'.

Paul castigated Christian communities who met 'to eat the Lord's Supper' while they were divided. 'I am told that when you meet as a congregation, you fall into sharply divided groups.'

The social development of medieval and post-medieval Europe gave the Church and its liturgy a central unifying role in the integrated community to which the Church was central. In the small communities of villages and small towns, the relationship between all their members was the expression of the integrated social structure of the people. The teacher, the parson, the doctor, the smith, the farmer, the merchant, the innkeeper, all had their integrating part to play. People met one another throughout the week in the course of their normal 'secular lives'. And on Sundays, the liturgy of the people expressed a real and actual sense of community. The traditions of the community were guarded by the liturgical sequence of the Book of Common Prayer. The blessing of the plough on Rogation Day, and at a later date the Thanksgiving for Harvest, prayers for rain during drought, or fine weather during continuous storm, and so on, tied the prayer and worship of the Church to the common daily concerns of the whole community. The rubrics of the Prayer Book for services relating to baptisms, marriages, thanksgiving for childbirth, and death, all presuppose their per-formance within a community.

The offices of Morning and Evening Prayer were announced by the sounding of the church bell daily. On Sundays the community was represented by a team of bellringers whose skill has created a tradition of campanology which is more highly developed in England than anywhere else in the world.

The Industrial Revolution and the population and urbanisation explosion which followed it has changed that simple community basis of liturgy. The word 'community' is used far too lightly today in speaking of our cities and parishes. The most basic human community of all – the family – is itself under pressure, not only from weakened moral standards, but from the migration of young people in search of better employment opportunities. Community consciousness is more likely to be within those who share a common professional or occupational interest. The local 'pub' in England is more representative of a sense of community than the church. Working-men's clubs or the local sports clubs draw people together in a type of cultural community far more than does any initiative of the local church. Travel is so much easier now that a congregation in a church on Sunday may travel for many miles from their homes. The people they meet in church may not be met again in any community context until the following Sunday. Social life flourishes outside the activities of the Church. The social unity of Paul's Church which expressed itself naturally in the breaking of bread is not generally evident in our Christian society today.

What, then, remains of a co-ordinated spiritual discipline, since liturgy no longer relates, as once it did, to the corporate habits of a definable community? The Christian calendar has been so invaded by commercial exploitation that even the great festivals of Christmas and Easter are hard put to it to retain their essential Christian character. The ancient insights of 'Mothering Sunday' are sentimentalised in 'Mother's Day' which retains little reference to its original meaning of our love for 'Mother Church'. 'Father's Day' has been invented by the greeting-card and gift manufacturers to make a meaningless distinction between parents. Lent is observed less and less, at a time when the need for self-discipline becomes more and more urgent. The pressure of the daily routine and sheer physical fatigue has made private prayer the practice of the persevering few, and even these are not helped by the preference for sermons on morality and current affairs when Christians are hungry for instruction in the prayer life. The considerable increase in Bible-reading resulting from new translations of the Scriptures is evidence of the deep-seated concern to be informed about the basics of Christian belief, but the regular teaching practices of the local church have to contend with difficulties – travel, fatigue and television – in gathering groups together during the week.

While acknowledging that a great deal is patiently and faithfully happening here and there, especially in the new suburbs, to increase the teaching opportunities of the Church, it is not cynical to say that, on the whole, all that remains of the spiritual character of the integrated community of past centuries is 'going to church' on Sunday morning. Furthermore, those who go to church are mainly those who are still living on the training in prayer and a knowledge of the Bible which they received in childhood. We are passing into a future in which their children and their children's children seem likely to lack such training and will be less and less able to participate in meaningful worship.

The passionate sense of idealism which, in a wide range of activities, is evident in the lives of the young generation today is ready for a relevant and meaningful foundation of belief and discipline. The frustration of the student generation in the field of politics is the result of their lack of confidence in the integrity and the objectives of those who lead them.

The demonstration which took place so violently at the Democratic Convention in Chicago in 1968 was a protest against the vacuum of ineptitude in political leadership, but it was also a cry for leadership. No generation in the past has responded more than would the present generation to a clear statement of ideals based on a coherent statement of belief. Only after accepting the integrity of a statement of belief would they readily accept the discipline required to translate that belief into ideals. A meaningful renewal of belief, a consequent definition of ideals worth working for, and a willing acceptance of discipline remain the conditions by which Christians could provide leadership today, as they have been the conditions of effective Christian leadership in the past.

It is, however, the provision of an effective medium through which Christians can learn their belief, define their ideals and see the reason for discipline, which has been lacking in the Church at the local level during the past half century of change in religious practice. As has been said, 'going to church' is largely all that remains of what was once a Christian presence in the whole community.

The Early Church, as we saw in the sentence already quoted, met 'to hear the apostles teach, to share the common life, to break bread and to *pray*'.

At the heart of a meeting of those who are conscious of coming together in the name and in the service of God is a deep instinct to pray; not merely to 'say prayers', but in a deep sense to have communion with God through the common experience of their communion one with another. This sense of communion with one another is founded upon a sense of need for one another. Each person in the company has a need for the support, love and understanding of every other individual in the company. Self-sufficiency and arrogance prohibit the spirit of prayer because they deny need, either for others or for God.

The need starts in the inner awareness of the individual of his or her own frailty. The weakness that is in each one is continually striving to be redeemed by the potential strength that is also in each one. The conscious awareness of the inner struggle between our weakness and our strength is the first awareness of the practice of prayer.

The Czech Marxist philosopher Marcovec, in wrestling with his attempt to understand the meaning of prayer, uses the jargon of Marxism in a way which enlightens the inner struggle from which prayer begins. It is to him 'the inner dialectic between a man and his inner self' – the inner creative tension between the two natures of a man. The two natures may be variously defined: animal – moral, natural – supernatural, physical – spiritual. To ignore this – in whatever form we choose to ignore it – may be represented as 'scientific', but it flies in the face of the evidence of conflict which consciousness of one's 'self' reveals to the man who honestly interprets his experience. To ignore the tension of the 'inner dialectic' is to destroy the balance of personality which depends upon acknowledgement of both parts of it within us – the good and the evil, the true and the false, the idealistic and the base. To acknowledge the tension is to have taken the first step towards reconciling it.

Among its achievements, prayer enables a conscious communication within oneself of the two natures of man. It was while the Psalmist 'kept silence, even from good words' that eventually 'the fire kindled' and he 'spake with his tongue'. Our speech is too ready. Too often it glides comfortably over the struggle within us. The struggle may demand 'sweat like great drops of blood falling to the ground' as in the 'dialectic' of the two choices of Jesus in Gethsemane A spoken prayer, be it in the language of the most majestic of Cranmer's collects, will not of itself create the inner consciousness of prayer. The consciousness of the inner conversation within a man between his two natures is an experience of the structure of prayer. When a man has understood that prayer, at this inner lever, is an inescapable and natural part of his being, he is more likely to put meaning into prayers spoken formally on his behalf.

To conduct the dialogue, or to direct the 'dialectic', within the privacy of one's heart, soon drives us to draw on the experience of others. The Psalmist who knew joy and sorrow, and had the profound insight to write:

> If I climb up into heaven thou art there:
> If I go down to hell, thou art there also:

has left us a treasury of spiritual experience which will meet every need of comfort or understanding. No less do we draw strength from the writings of others who have recorded their own experienced prayers. Bonhoeffer has in our times enlightened the struggle of millions by the faithful recording of his own. The Bible itself is for us, at moments when we are drawn to the experience of the prayers of others, an inexhaustible source of strength. It records the insights of those who recognised the tension in themselves, in their community life, and in the history of their nation as they regarded it.

As the inner prayer of a man is an inescapable and natural part of his being, so is his leaning towards the spiritual experience of others a natural part of his being.

The meeting of the Christian community in a church, in a home or wherever 'two or three are gathered together' must, as a mark of its essential validity as a Christian community, be able naturally and effectively to provide for this need to share the common experience of awareness of the inner dialectic of prayer which is in every man. To acknowledge our need to make creative the inner dialectic in each one individually is the first step in prayer. To share this need with others who acknowledge it in themselves and wish to experience it corporately is the second. Then personally, corporately and universally we will acknowledge the reality of God as the other partner in our prayer because he alone can fulfil the need which is in us.

We cannot love God unless we love our neighbours. We love our neighbours when we are capable of embracing them in the communion of prayer. Love of this kind is the accurate assessment of the needs of the person loved, and the openheartedness available to meet those needs. That is the love God has for us, and makes available to us when we acknowledge our need to him in prayer. But we cannot understand it, nor be ready to receive it until we have practised it in a love − prayer relationship with our neighbours.

When the new Coventry Cathedral was being built, a team of men and women was drawn together to design the future ministry to be associated with the new building which had been designed architecturally with vision and genius. The building was born and nurtured in the controversy which was inevitable in the mere fact that it was new in concept. It was a controversy too, however, at a deeper level than that. There were many who questioned the wisdom of building a cathedral at all in the twentieth century. Deep in their uneasiness was a more profound question as to the relevance of religion itself in modern society. Coventry city was taken by many to symbolise all that is modern, efficient and self-confident in our world. The apparent irrelevance of religion in a city of progress and achievement seemed to be emphasised in the building of a cathedral at its centre.

Those brought together to bring the building to life were deeply conscious of this honest questioning. It became an important part of their own. What, essentially, has religion got to give to modern society which modern society cannot do without? Only absolute honesty could answer that question, even to the extent of facing bitter criticism from those in the traditional areas of the Church's life who did not

acknowledge the question. The continued probing of
the ministry of the Coventry team into new areas of
ministry in the secular city is a continuous process of
proving the answer — that religion is to a secular
society what man's spiritual-moral consciousness is
to his body. In other words, the team has recognised
the 'two-dimensionality' of corporate life in human
society, and has based all its striving for an effective
ministry on the assumption that the dialectic between
the 'sacred' and the 'secular' is creative and essential.

This acknowledgement provided the character for
the foundation relationship between members of the
team — a relationship of prayer, the inner
communion, within each member individually, among
all members corporately, among all who form the
congregational fellowship of the cathedral, and then,
meaningfully, between all these together and
Almighty God.

The honesty which has resulted has been born of
an honestly accepted weakness. Only those who do
not acknowledge weakness and need, hide their
weakness by calling it strength. The first fruit of real
prayer, either in the silence of one's own privacy, or
in Bible-study at a meeting of the team or any other
group, or in a really praying congregation, is honesty
about oneself. Honesty about oneself is the first
condition of being able to pray to God to meet one's
weakness with his strength.

The search for a new spirituality to enlarge the
minimal observance of 'going to church' has led the
ministry of the new cathedral in Coventry to examine
other restatements of Christian spirituality in

104

previous periods of history when the Church has found the same need for renewal. Notable among these have been the Benedictine Rule and the Rule of the Taizé Community.

From this examination of what others have found helpful, and the urgent sense of need in the situation in which Coventry Cathedral is called to serve, a statement of the Common Discipline has been evolved, which sets down the intentions and the methods by which the spiritual values may be nourished in lives fully aware of their contemporary duties. This is reproduced in full at the end of this chapter.

The membership of the Discipline is not made public; no question of first or second-class Christians is raised. All members of the staff are able to accept the spirit of the Discipline as it is defined in the 'Corporate Meditation'.

The practice of the Discipline itself adds very little to the sort of discipline which any ordered life undertakes. It merely clarifies it, and makes it more explicit. All those who have undertaken to adhere to it testify to the enrichment of their lives which this common order has produced. Particularly relevant is the commitment to disciplined attendance at corporate worship, the commitment to regular study, and the system of *foyers*.

The word *foyer* means *hearth*. The image suggested is of a family group gathered around the fireside. Its centre is the common meal. The *foyers* are selected 'out of a hat' every six months. Each consists of seven members. The meeting of three hours, including a meal, takes place in the homes of each in turn, once every month. The meal is of the simplest so as to avoid competing with each other. The groups so arranged succeed in bringing together members of the staff, senior and junior, who seldom meet in relaxed conversation. The meeting has no theme, far less an agenda. Many a meeting has inhibited the freely moving guidance of the Spirit by the constriction of an agenda. The staff of Coventry Cathedral unanimously testify to the central value of the meetings of the *foyers*.

The value of such relaxed groups in a congregation cannot be overestimated. Those who see one another in church seldom have opportunities to meet one another as relaxed persons, if they meet at all. Some meet in vestries, others in formal study groups, but seldom if ever do they meet with the relaxed friendship which is supremely becoming to Christian people. The Coventry Staff Discipline is now being applied, with suitable and obvious modifications, to the large congregation who belong to the Cathedral family. It has been immediately recognised that the heart of the success of the discipline for the congregation is to be found in the *foyers*. The chaplain to the congregation selects 'out of the hat' the names of those who will comprise the groups of seven. The first name on the list of each group merely undertakes to call together the groups to arrange the dates and places of each meeting. New friendships and understandings are created, love in the true Christian sense is set free, and the strength which is engendered in each group rapidly enriches the relationships between all members of the congregation.

Then the liturgy on Sunday morning becomes warm and meaningful. The achievement may be thought to be modest, and so it is. But its alternative is the continuance of the present barrenness and formality which mocks the warm Christian love in action. New visions emerge and new adventures in discipleship are defined.

We stand at what could become one of the great creative moments in Christian history. It will become so if we structure our Church life on and set our direction from the experience of a new discovery of love for one another. Starting at that point, we shall begin a journey to a future in which the Church will be a meaningful influence in a society which is bewildered and broken, and the first direction of our effort to renew the Church will be towards a new spirituality.

APPENDIX

The 'Common Discipline' of Coventry Cathedral

I. THE SPIRIT OF THE DISCIPLINE

IN THE SIXTH CENTURY St. Benedict founded the Order which still carries his name. Within the tradition of St. Basil, John Cassian and others, he initiated a movement of reform which speaks clearly to our present condition at Coventry Cathedral.

a. Benedict, Patron of Europe

This proud designation, authorised by the Pope, engenders large thoughts. Benedict lived in the dark age which followed the break-up of the Roman Empire, the fragmentation of Western culture and civilisation. His movement recaptured for Europe a measure of stability and graciousness. Today European cultural, political and economic dominance is in decline. Her true hope lies in her becoming united, not in an attempt to re-establish that dominance but so that her still vast resources of capital and technical skill may be the more rapidly and effectively applied to the needs of the developing nations south and east of her. In the progressive realisation of this destiny for Europe lies the particular, if modest, vocation of Coventry Cathedral.

b. Benedict, Creator of a lay spirituality

In an age when the 'religious' life was practised largely by the heroically ascetic, Benedict devised a compassionate, if still tough rule for laymen, most of whom were of peasant stock. We too need to seek from God a new spirituality for the whole people of God.

Coventry Cathedral staff is composed of clergy and laity and of married and unmarried members in approximately equal proportions. A common discipline for us of work and prayer would not only sustain us but might be of wider application as the churches move into an era characterised by team and group ministries.

c. Benedict, Dweller in mountain

Benedict built his 'eyrie' on Monte Cassino. His successors sought locations far from the cities but with abundant water, places of peace and natural beauty. Our Midland Cathedral, threatened by engulfment in a vast conurbation stretching continuously from Liverpool to Dover, is called to promote a subtly scientific ecology which will allow forms of animal and plant life other than human to flourish in our land.

d. Benedict, Master of corporate worship

For Benedict corporate worship was the *Opus Dei*. For us too, corporate worship must lie at the heart of our common discipline.

IN THE ELEVENTH CENTURY a great Benedictine Abbey began to be constructed on the site occupied by the new Coventry Cathedral. This construction symbolises not only our continuity with the mainstream of Benedictine tradition but also our primary vocation to local and worldwide mission. The history of the Benedictine Order can be told in terms of an interchange of mission between what were in process of becoming the nations of Europe.

IN THE SIXTEENTH CENTURY this Abbey was destroyed as a consequence of the Reformation. This destruction symbolises a proper discontinuity with the Benedictine tradition and warns us against any sentimental attachment to the past. Like St. Paul before him, Luther wrestled with law and rule and sounded the clarion call of 'justification by faith'. And so we speak and seek to enact not a common rule but a common 'discipline' – a word which retains something of the strength of a rule but also something of the liberty of a way of life, a discipleship. Luther also married a wife as did other reformers. Marriage radically refashions the loyalty to the work, fidelity to the spouse and stewardship of possessions. Our discipline must reflect this refashioning.

110

IN THE TWENTIETH CENTURY the new Coventry Cathedral was built. It is a product of our technological age. This age is characterised among Christians and others by a widespread disenchantment with the supernatural, and observable shift of emphasis, for better or for worse, from worship of the mysterious God to service of him in our neighbour. Our urban society is also characterised by a separation of our homes from our places of work. Whereas the prized Benedictine *stabilitas* was and is based on a common home, our fellowship is rather a fellowship of common work. Certainly we are called to a discipline of worship and prayer. Yet that which has brought us together and constitutes our community is a shared work. And this must be reflected in our discipline, our *Opus Dei*, with honesty and without guilt, if it is to be a discipline, common to all who join our staff.

Our age is also characterised by an emphasis on planning, that is, a rational attempt to relate activity, to define aims. Our fellowship, therefore, is to be a fellowship of theological thought and action, a rational attempt to implement shared theological insights.

Another feature of our age is the replacement of the autocratic forms of government which prevailed in Benedict's day and for many centuries, by more democratic forms which, whether or not they have divine sanction, are more appropriate to a society in which education is universal. So the relationship between Provost and Staff is radically different from that between Abbot and monks. An analogy of our

111

working relationship may be sought rather in the relationship between an English Prime Minister and his Cabinet colleagues. Our common loyalty is to the work and to God.

FOR CORPORATE MEDITATION

We have acknowledged our debt to the ancient, catholic tradition of St. Benedict, a tradition that was nurtured in the womb of the undivided Church. We are distinctively called to a ministry of reconciliation. It is right, therefore, for us now to turn to a contemporary reformed spirituality dedicated to the reuniting of that Church of God. The quotations which follow from the Rule of Taizé contribute to our common discipline as an inspiration for our corporate meditation.

1. Assured of your salvation by the unique grace of our Lord Jesus Christ, you do not impose discipline on yourself for its own sake. Gaining mastery of yourself has no other aim than to render you more available. Let there be no useless asceticism; hold only to the works God commands. To carry the burdens of others, accepting the petty injuries of each day, so as to share concretely in the sufferings of Christ; this is our first discipline.

2. Be a sign of joy and of brotherly love among men. Open yourself to all that is human and you will see any vain desire to flee from the world vanish from

your heart. Be present to the time in which you live; adapt yourself to the conditions of the moment. 'Father, I pray thee, not to take them out of the world, but to keep them from evil.'

3. Love your neighbour, whatever may be his political or religious beliefs. Never resign yourself to the scandal of the separation of Christians, all who so readily confess love for their neighbour, and yet remain divided. Be consumed with burning zeal for the unity of the Body of Christ.

4. Let us be attentive to enter into the meaning of the liturgical action; let us seek to perceive under signs accessible to our fleshly being something of the invisible reality of the Kingdom. But let us also take care not to multiply these signs and to keep them simple, the token of their evangelical worth.

5. Common prayer does not dispense us from personal prayer. The one sustains the other. Each day, let us take time aside to renew our personal intimacy with Jesus Christ.

6. Nothing is more harmful to objective judgment than the ties born of particular preferences, for we may risk agreeing with a Brother, hoping perhaps unconsciously to win his occasional support in return. Nothing is more contrary to the spirit of the discipline than a search which is not purified by the sole desire to discern God's will.

7. For your prayer to be real, you must be at grips with hard work. If you were to remain a *dilettante*, you would be incapable truly to intercede. Your prayer will become total when it is one with your work.

8. Interior silence renders possible our conversation with Jesus Christ. But who does not fear this silence, and prefer diversions at the hour of work; and would not rather flee from prayer by tiring himself in vain tasks, forgetful of his neighbour and of himself?

9. Buffoonery has never renewed joy. Let us remember that there is no sharp dividing line between frank humour and irony which turns a smile into a grimace. Mockery — that poison of common life — is treacherous because under its cover are flung the so-called truths one dare not say face to face; it is cowardly because it ruins the person of a Brother before the others.

10. As peace with Christ implies peace with your neighbour, be reconciled and make amends where possible. Forgive your brother until seventy times seven.

11. Nothing divides so much as continual discussions about everything and nothing. Know, if need be, how to put an end to them. Refuse to listen to insinuations concerning one or another Brother. Be a ferment of unity.

12. It is Christ himself whom we receive in a guest. Let us learn to welcome; let us be willing to offer our leisure time; let hospitality be liberal and exercised with discernment.

13. With the growing number of visitors, we run into the danger of cutting ourselves off from them, by reclusion in order to defend ourselves. On the contrary, while preserving our deeper life, keeping a certain discernment and avoiding feverish dissipation, let us remember on every occasion how to be open and hospitable.

People who come to us expect bread, and if we present them with stones to look at, we shall have fallen short in our ecumenical vocation. They seek in us men who radiate God. This implies a life hidden in God, so that the presence of Christ which is borne by each Brother, may be renewed within us.

14. The expectation which is shown towards us is very demanding. What is expected of us is that we be consistent in our ecumenical vocation; men seeking unity in all things, to show forth fellowship in their daily life.

15. There is a sign of contradiction to those who have received an ecumenical vocation. From then on we are sometimes placed in opposition and it is understandable that we support this trial with difficulty. It may become intolerable, giving rise without our knowledge to reactions of fear,

sometimes even sorrow. Therefore, we are called to unite, to be men of peace with all men, and particularly with our Brothers who belong to the same confessional family.

16. We are submitted to heavy tensions which can only grow; in the Church where the resistance to change opposes our ecumenical and missionary vocation; and in a world where rapid evolution ceaselessly endangers peace. It occurs sometimes that we are signs of contradiction to the point of being able to say: 'Long enough have I been dwelling with those who hate peace. I am for peace, but when I speak they are for fighting.' (Ps. 120) Then it remains for us to bless, to invoke peace for all men, and in order to do that to keep peace in spirit and body, to seek refuge and to repose in God's peace.

17. Apathy and carelessness inevitably lead to sadness and lukewarmness. Due to common life, some Brothers occasionally bear more work and cares than others, whereas we all must be exposed to the tension which is found in the very nature of our work.

18. The very overburdening of our ministry must continually render more density to our common prayer. We could not lengthen it very much; therefore let us aim to be as completely present as possible during this prayer, where all things are entrusted to God. The balance of our life is conditioned by our attention to worship.

19. Love solitude but loathe isolation.

20. Contemplation braces our love for God. If it is authentic this affection of our whole being for Christ is bound to be an outgoing expression towards our neighbour. And the love we bear to our neighbour remains the mark of true contemplation.

21. At every advance of age in our life, we are asked for an inner rejuvenescence. As we grow older let us preserve a youthful spirit and mind which is invigorated in our continual openness to important evolutions in the world and in the Church, by accepting also what is new, through our wonderment in facing each today of God.

22. Man to man transparency does not mean to pour out one's heart, but limpidity of the whole person.

23. We may accomplish works worthy of admiration, yet the only ones that will count are the ones which rise from the merciful love of Christ in us. In the evening of our life, we shall be judged by the love and charity which we have let grow and expand, little by little, in mercy for every man living, in the Church and in the world.

24. 'A School of the Lord's Service'
    'We have, therefore, to establish a school of the Lord's service in the setting forth of which we hope to order nothing that is harsh or rigorous. But if anything be somewhat strictly laid down according to

117

the dictates of sound reason, for the amendment of vices or the preservation of charity, do not therefore fly in dismay from the way of salvation, whose beginning cannot but be strait and difficult. But as we go forward in our life and in faith, we shall with hearts enlarged and unspeakable sweetness of love run in the way of God's commandments; so that never departing from His guidance, but persevering in His teaching until death, we may deserve to be partakers of His Kingdom'. (From the Prologue to the Rule of St. Benedict. Translated by the Abbot of Fort Augustus.)

25. 'You, my friends, were called to be free men; only do not turn your freedom into licence for your lower nature but be servants to one another in love. For the whole law can be summed up in a single commandment: 'Love your neighbour as yourself.'

'But the harvest of the Spirit is love, joy, peace, patience, kindness, goodness, fidelity, gentleness, and self control. If the Spirit is the source of our life, let the Spirit also direct our course'.

'We must not be conceited, challenging one another to rivalry, jealous of one another. If a man should do something wrong, my brothers, on a sudden impulse, you who are endowed with the Spirit must set him right again very gently. Look to yourself each one of you; you may be tempted too. Help one another to carry these heavy loads, and in this way you will fulfil the law of Christ'. 'For if a man

imagines himself to be somebody, when he is nothing, he is deluding himself. Each man should examine his own conduct for himself; then he can measure his achievement by comparing with himself and not with anyone else. For everyone has his own proper burden to bear' (St. Paul's Letter to the Christians in Galatia 5. 13, 14, 22, 26; 6. 1 − 5).
Quotations are taken from the English Edition of the Rule of Taize, published by the Faith Press, with acknowledgements.)

11. THE PRACTICE OF THE DISCIPLINE

1. The Work of God

Of the one hundred and sixty eight hours in the week members of the discipline allot a minimum of one third, that is fifty six hours, to work, study, worship and prayer. Of this not less than five hours in any week shall be allotted to prayer and worship and not less than five hours to study. Members decide for themselves what constitutes work, study, prayer, and worship. They are, of course, at liberty substantially to exceed the minimum periods in any week. Members attend the celebration of the Holy Communion, breakfast, Bible Study and staff meetings on Mondays whenever possible. Members excuse themselves to the Provost or to whomever he appoints for this purpose when they expect to be absent. Members also endeavour to attend Morning Prayer from Monday to Friday.

2. Recreation and Holidays

Whenever possible members take a whole day off work each week. Married members, whenever possible, spend some time each day in recreation with members of their families and are not to neglect their families under pressure of work. Other members who do not live alone define their own obligations towards members of their households. Members normally take in full the annual holidays allotted to the staff. When on holiday or otherwise away from the Cathedral, they observe the spirit of the Discipline.

3. Sleep, Food, and Drink

Members provide time for sufficient sleep for good health and neither eat nor drink to excess. Unless prevented by illness or other good cause, they abstain from one meal a week and give the money thus saved to the poor.

4. Money

Members draw up an annual budget of their income and expenditure, to include such items as: direct giving; food, clothing; recreation and holidays; hospitality; transport; insurance.

5. Consultants

Each member shall have a Consultant who should normally be a member of the Discipline. He and his Consultant will arrange to meet from time to time for a relaxed discussion of the observance of the

Discipline and any other matters he may wish. At this point the language of confession and spiritual direction is carefully avoided. The Discipline is made for the members and not the members for the Discipline. Each member informs the Provost, or whom he may designate, whom he had invited to act as his Consultant. These arrangements are without prejudice to the right of all members to consult each other at any time.

6. Common Meals

In addition to breakfast together on Monday mornings members take a meal together four or five times every six months in smaller groups, with not more than seven members in each. Every such meal is accompanied by a period of open talk, the whole occasion lasting for not less than two hours. Members act in turn as hosts and do not vie with each other to provide other than homely hospitality. The Provost, or whom he delegates for this purpose, selects new groups at Easter and Michaelmas. The hostess on any occasion is most welcome to attend but need not.

7. Relationship to the Bishop, to the Cathedral Congregation and to other Cathedrals and Collegiate Churches.

On behalf of the members the Provost shall consult with the Bishop as to a proper association of the Bishop with the Discipline as Guardian of its observance. In particular, members have access to the Bishop for pastoral, personal and spiritual advice.

Members earnestly hope to discover a proper form of association with the Discipline members of the Cathedral Congregation. They recognise that this may in due course mean revision of the Discipline.

Members also hope that such Discipline may encourage other Cathedrals and Collegiate Churches to express their collegiality in new ways. Here again they recognise that it may be right to revise their Discipline in such a way as to secure a Discipline commonly acceptable to other bodies.

8. Revision of the Disciplines

The Staff holds an annual Conference outside Coventry for at least forty-eight and if possible up to seventy-two hours. At this Conference the first item on the agenda is an opportunity to revise the Discipline. At the same time the Provost announces fresh groupings for the Common Meal for the following year. Decisions as to revision are obtained by the normal methods of staff consultation. Any revisions must be precisely worded when they are agreed.

9. Memberships

Adherence to the spirit of the Discipline is normally expected of the 'Monday morning Staff'. If any member has reservations about such adherence, he or she is asked, as a courtesy, to inform the Provost by letter. Commitment to the practice of the Discipline is open equally to all members of the 'Monday morning Staff'. Those who so commit themselves inform the Provost by letter. Prospective members of staff receive a copy of the Common Discipline before appointment, and after their arrival are invited by the Provost to commit themselves, if they wish, to the practice of the Discipline.

10. Recollection of the Discipline

The Discipline is read out to the members, section by section, or as the Provost shall arrange; provided that the whole is read through at least twice in any one calendar year.

11. Wives of Members, and Former Members of Staff

Wives of members are invited to accept the spirit of the Discipline. Those who do so are asked to inform the Provost or whomever he appoints for this purpose. On leaving the Cathedral Staff, members will be assumed to cease to be members of the Discipline unless circumstances enable them to ask to continue to be associated with it in a meaningful way, in which case they inform the Provost.